THE

CONSTITUTION,

AND LAWS

OF THE

CHOCTAW NATION.

PRINTED AT DOAKSVILLE, 1852.

Scholarly Resources Inc.
1508 Pennsylvania Avenue · Wilmington, Delaware 19806

SCHOLARLY RESOURCES, INC.
Wilmington, Delaware • London

Reprint edition published in 1975

Library of Congress Catalog Card Number: 75-3682
ISBN: 0-8420-1848-4

Manufactured in the United States of America

THE
CONSTITUTION,
AND LAWS
OF THE
CHOCTAW NATION.

PRINTED AT DOAKSVILLE, 1852.

THE

CONSTITUTION,

AND LAWS

OF THE

CHOCTAW NATION.

PRINTED AT DOAKSVILLE, 1852.

WE, the people of the Choctaw Nation, having the right to establish our own form of Government, not inconsistent with the Constitution, Treaties and Laws of the United States, by our own Representatives assembled in Convention at Nanihwaiya, on Monday the 14th of October, 1850.

In order to establish justice, insure tranquility, promote the general welfare and secure to ourselves and our posterity the right of life, liberty and property, we mutually agree with each other, to form for ourselves, a free and independent Government—and we do hereby recognize the boundaries assigned the Choctaw Nation, by the second article of the treaty made and concluded with the United States of America, at Dancing Rabbit Creek, on the 27th of September, 1830, viz: Beginning near Fort Smith where the Arkansas boundary crosses the Arkansas river, running thence to the source of the Canadian, if in the limits of the United States, or to those limits; thence due South to Red river, thence down Red river to the Western boundary of the State of Arkansas, thence North along the line to the beginning; the boundary of the same to be agreeable to the treaty made and concluded at Washington City in the year 1825.

District Boundaries.

For the convenience and good government of the people of the Choctaw Nation, we make and ordain and establish four Districts in this Nation to be known by the following names and boundaries, viz: Mosholatubbee District, Pushmataha District, Chickasaw District and Apukshanubbee District

The boundary line of Mosholatubbee District shall begin near Fort Smith, where the Arkansas boundary crosses the Arkansas river, thence up said river to the Canadian Fork, to where the Chickasaw District boundary strikes the same, thence along the said Chickasaw District boundary to where it strikes the Dividing Ridge, between the Canadian and Red rivers, thence eastwardly along said Dividing Ridge to the Western boundary of the State of Arkansas, thence along said Arkansas line to the beginning.

The boundary of Apukshanubbee District shall begin on Red river, where the Arkansas State line strikes the same, running thence up said river to the mouth of Kiamishi, thence up said river to Jacks Fork, thence up said Jacks Fork to the military road, leading from Fort Smith to Horse Prairie, thence along said military road to the boundary line of Mosholatubbee District on the top of the Dividing Ridge between the Arkansas and Red rivers, thence Eastwardly along said District boundary to the Western boundary of the State of Arkansas to the beginning.

The boundary of Pushmataha District shall begin on Red river at the mouth of Kiamishi, thence running up said Red river to the mouth of Island Bayou to where the Chickasaw District boundary strikes said river, agreeably to the provisions of the Treaty made and concluded between the Choctaws and Chickasaws at Doaksville, in the year 1837.—Thence along said Chickasaw District boundary to the Dividing Ridge between the Canadian and Red rivers, thence Eastwardly to the line of Mosholatubbee on the top of the Dividing Ride, to where the District line of Apukshanubbee District intersects Mosholatubbee District, thence South along said Apukshanubbee District line to the beginning.

The Chickasaw District shall be bounded as follows, viz: Beginning on the North Bank of Red river at the mouth of Island Bayou about eight or ten miles below the mouth of False Washita, thence running North along the main channel of said bayou to its source, along the Dividing Ridge to the road leading from Fort Gibson to Fort Washita, thence along said road to the line dividing Mosholatubbee and Pushmataha District, thence Eastwardly along said District line to the source of Brushy creek, thence down said creek to where it flows into the Canadian, thence West along said Canadian river to its source, if in the limits of the United States, and thence due South to Red river and down Red river to the beginning.

The General Council shall have the power by law to subdivide the several Districts of this Nation into as many counties as may be deemed necessary for the convenience of holding County Courts, Elections and for other purposes.

ARTICLE II.

Declaration of Rights.

SEC. 1. All freemen when they form a Social Compact are equal in rights; and no man, or set of men, are entitled to exclusive, separate public emoluments or privileges but in consideration of public services.

SEC. 2. All political power is inherent in the people, and free governments are founded on their authority, and instituted for their benefit; and therefore they may have, at all times, an inalienable and indefeasable right to alter, reform or abolish their form of Government in such manner as they may think expedient.

SEC. 3. There shall be no establishment of religion by law. No preference shall ever be given by law to any religious sect, society, denomination or mode of worship, and no religious test shall ever be allowed as a qualification to any public trust under this Government.

SEC. 4. No human authority ought, in any case whatever, to control or interfere with the rights of conscience.

SEC. 5. No person shall for the same offence be twice put in jeopardy of life or limbs, nor shall any person's property be taken or applied to any public use unless just compensation be made therefor.

SEC. 6. No title of nobility or hereditary distinction, privileges, honor or emoluments shall ever be granted or conferred under this Government, nor shall any office be created, the appointment of which shall be for a longer time than during good behavior.

SEC. 7. The right of trial by jury shall remain inviolate

SEC. 8. Every citizen has a right to bear arms in defence of himself and his country.

SEC. 9. That the printing press shall be free to every person, and no law shall ever be made to restrain the rights thereof. The free communication of opinions is one of the inviolable rights of man, and every citizen may freely speak, write and print on any subject, being responsible for the abuse of that liberty.

SEC. 10. That the people shall be secure in their persons, houses, papers and possessions from unreasonable searchers and seizures. And that general warrants whereby any officer may be commanded to search suspected places without evidence of the fact committed, or to seize any person or persons not named whose offences are not particularly described, and supported by evidences, are dangerous to liberty and shall not be granted. But in all cases where suspicion rests on any person, or persons of conviving, or secreting whiskey or other intoxicating liquors, the same shall be liable to search or seizure as may be hereinafter provided by law.

SEC. 11. That no freemen shall be taken or imprisoned, or disseized of his free hold liberties or privilege, or outlawed, or exiled, or in any manner destryed or deprived of his life, liberty and property, but by the judgment of his peers or the law of the land.

SEC. 12. That in all criminal prosecutions the accused hath the right to be heard by himself and counsel, to demand the nature and causes of the accusation against him, and have a copy thereof to meet the witness face to face, to have compulsory for obtaining witnesses in his favor. And in prosecutions by indictment or presentment, a speedy public trial, by an impartial jury of the county or district in which the crime shall have been committed, and shall not be compelled to give evidence against himself.

SEC. 13. That all penalties shall be reasonable and proportioned to the nature of the offence.

SEC. 14. That the citizens have a right in a peaceable manner to assemble together for their common good to instruct their Representatives and apply to those invested with the power of the Government, for a redress of grievances or other proper purposes by address or remonstrance.

SEC. 15. There shall be no retrospective law, or any law passed under this Constitution, imparing the obligations of contracts.

ARTICLE III.

Distribution of powers.

SEC. 1. The powers of the Government of the Choctaw Nation. shall be divided into three distinct departments, and each of them confined to a separate body of magistracy, viz: Those which are legislative to one, those which are executive to another, and those which are judicial to another.

SEC. 2. No person or collection of persons, being one of those departments shall exercise any power properly belonging to either of the others except in the instances hereafter expressly directed or permitted by the General Council.

ARTICLE IV.

Legislative Department.

SEC. 1. The legislative power of this Nation shall be vested in a General Council, which shall consist of a Senate and House of Representatives, and the style of their laws shall be: "*Be it enacted by the General Council of the Choctaw Nation assembled.*"

SEC. 2. The Senate of the Choctaw Nation shall be composed of four Senators from each District, chosen by the qualified electors for the term of two years.

SEC. 3. No person shall be Senator who shall not have

attained the age of thirty years, and been one year a citizen of this Nation, and who shall not, when elected, be an inhabitant of that district for which he shall be chosen.

Sec. 4. No person shall be a Senator unless he be an acknowledge citizen of this Nation.

Sec. 5. The Senate shall choose a President from its own body, who shall have no vote unless they be equally divided.

Sec. 6. The Senate shall choose its other officers.

Sec. 7. The General Council shall have the sole power to try all impeachments. When sitting for that purpose, they shall be on oath or affirmation to do justice according to law and evidence, and no person shall be convicted without the concurrence of two thirds of both branches of the General Council.

Sec. 8. Judgement in cases of impeachment shall not extend further than removal from office; but the parties charged with any crime, shall nevertheless, before or after impeachment, be liable to indictment, trial judegment and punishment according to law; and when charges for impeachment are preferred, the person or persons so charged shall be duly notified by the light-horsemen, by order of the Cheif or Judge, to attend the General Council and be heard by himself and counsel, that his trial may be fair and impartial.

Sec. 9, The House of Representatives shall be composed of members chosen every year by the qualified electors in the several Districts at the ratio of 1 Representative to every one thousand citizens, nevertheless, when there is a fractional, number of five hundred or more citizens in any District, they shall be entitled to one additional Representative. No person shall be a Representative unless he be an acknowledged citizen of the Choctaw Nation, or who shall not have attained the age of twenty-one years, or who shall not, when elected, be an inhabitant of that District in which he shall be chosen.

Sec. 10. In the case of death, resignation or inability of any of the Senators or Representatives from the several Districts, the executive shall have the power to make temporary appointments until the next election.

Sec. 11. Each House shall be the judge of the election returns and qualifications of its own members, and a majority of each Houses shall constitute a quorum to do business.

Sec. 12. Bills may originate in either House and be amended, altered or rejected by the other, and every bill shall be read on three different days in each House, unless two-thirds of the House, when the same is pending, shall dispense with the rules, but no bill shall have the force of a law, until it shall have been passed by a majority of both branches of the General Council, and every bill having passed both branches of the General Council shall be signed by the Speaker and Psesident of their respective bodies.

Sec. 13. Every bill which shall have passed the General Council shall be presented to the Chiefs or their Speaker; if they approve it, they shall sign it and it shall become a law; if not, they shall return it to the branch in which it originated, with their objections. The General Council shall then reconsider it, and if repassed by two-thirds of both branches it shall become a law as if the Chiefs had signed it.

Sec. 14. The House of Representatives, when assembled, shall choose a Speaker and its other officers, and when a majority of the members are assembled, it shall constitute a quorum to do business.

Sec. 15. The General Council may determine the rules of its own proceedings, and punish a member or other person for disorderly conduct or behavior, and shall keep a journal of its proceedings, and cause a true copy of the same to be sent to each district.

Sec. 16. The General Council of the Choctaw Nation shall assemble at least once in every year, and such meeting shall pe at Doaksville, on the first Wednesday in November, until altered by law. Nevertheless, the meeting of the General Council of 1850, shall be at Nanihwaiya.

Sec. 17. The yeas and nays of the members of the General Council, on any question shall, on the request of any three members present, be entered on the journal.

ARTICLE V.

Executive Department.

SEC. 1. The Supreme power of this Nation shall be vested in four District Chiefs, and any two ot them shall be deemed sufficient to exercise the duties of the Executive at the General Council.

SEC. 2. The Chiefs and their Speakers shall be elected the qualified electors within their respective districts, on the first Wednesday in August, 1854. And in case of death resignation, removal or ability of any of the Chiefs of the Nation, his Speaker shall exercise the duties of the Executive until a Chief shall be chosen at the next regular election, which Chief when elected, shall only serve out the remaining term.

SEC- 3. The present district Chiefs and their Speakers, shall remain in office and exercise the duties of their respective offices, until their successors shall be duly sworn into. office at the annual meeting of the General Council, in 1854

SEC. 4. The Chiefs and their Speakers shall hold their offiices for the term of four years from the time of their installation, until their successors shall be duly qualified, but they shall not be eligible for the same office for more than two terms in sucession.

SEC. 5. No person except a free and acknowledged citizen of the Choctaw Nation shall be eligible to the office of Chief or Speaker; neither shall any person be eligible to either of those offices, who shall not have attained to the age of thirty years and been an inhabitant of the Choctaw Nation at least one year.

SEC. 6. The Chiefs shall, from time to time, give to the General Council, information of the state of the Government, and recommend to their consideration such measures as they may deem expedient.

SEC. 7. They shall take care that the laws be faithfully executed.

SEC. 8. They may, by proclamation, on extraordinary occasions, convene the General Council at the seat of Government, or at a different place, if that shall have become, since their last adjournment, dangerous from an enemy or from contagious disease. In case of disagreement between the two Houses with respect to the time of adjournment, they may adjourn them to such a time as they shall think best, not beyond the day of the next meeting of the General Council.

SEC. 9. Vacancies that may happen in office, the election to which is vested in the General Council, shall be filled by the Chiefs in their respective districts, during the recess of the General Council, by granting commissions, which shall expire at the end of next session.

SEC. 10. The General Council shall have the power, by law, to determine the compensation of the Chiefs and Speakers.

SEC. 11. No person shall hold the office of district Chief and any other office, or commission, either in this Nation or under any State or in the United States, or under any other power at one and the same time.

SEC. 12. There shall be elected by the joint vote of both Houses of the General Council, an Auditor and Treasurer for each district, who shall hold the office for the term of two years, and until their respective successors are elected and qualified, unless sooner removed; and perform such duties as shall be prescribed by law; and in case of vacancy by death, resignation or otherwise, such vacancy shall be filled by the Chief of the district, as in other cases.

SEC. 13. The Chiefs and Speakers of the several districts, before they enter upon the duties of their office, shall take the following oath or affirmation, viz:

"I do solemnly swear [or affirm] that I will, to the best of my judgement and ability, faithful execute the duties of my office, and will preserve, protect and defend the Constitution of the Choctaw Nation."

SEC. 14. Each Chief ahall have the of appoint his district secretary, who shall act as clerk of the Circuit Court of the district, and shall receive such compensation and fees as the General Council may by law prescribe.

ARTICLE VI.

Judicial Department.

SEC. 1. The Judicial power of the Nation shall be vested

in a Supreme National Court, in District Circuit Courts and County Courts.

SEC. 2. The Supreme National Court shall be composed of four Judges, one to be chosen from each district; one of whom, shall be stiled Chief Justice; any three of whom shall constitute a quorum, and the concurrence of a majority of the judges presiding, shall in every case be necessary to a decision.

SEC 3. The Supreme National Court, except in cases otherwise directed by this Constitution, shall have appellate jurisdiction only, which shall be coextensive with the Nation, under such restrictions and regulations as may, from time to time, be prescribed by law.

SEC. 4. The District Circuit Court shall be composed of one Circuit Judge, and shall have original jurisdiction over all criminal cases which shall not be otherwise provided for by law, and exclusive original jurisdiction of all crimes amounting to felony, and original jurisdiction of all civil cases which shall not be cognazable before the Judges of the county, until otherwise directed by the General Council, and original jurisdiction in all matters of contract, and in all matters of controversy where the same is over fifty dollars.

It shall hold its term at such times and places in each district as may be by law directed.

SEC. 5. The Circuit Court shall exercise a superintending control over the County Courts, and shall have power to issue all the necessary writs to carry into effect their general and specific powers.

SEC. 6. The General Council, by joint vote of both Houses, shall elect the Judges of the Supreme National and Circuit Courts. A majority of the whole number in joint vote shall be necessary to a choice. The Judges of the Supreme National Court shall be at least thirty years of age, and shall hold their office during the term of four years from the date of their commission. The Judge of the Circuit Court be at least twenty-five years of age, and shall be elected for the term of two years from the date of his commission. The Supreme National Court shall appoint its own Clerk for the term of four years.

SEC 7. The Supreme National and Circuit Judges shall,

at stated times, receive a compensation for their services, to be determined by law, which shall not be diminished during the time for which they are elected. They shall not be allowed any fees or perquisites of office nor hold any other office of trust or profit under this Nation or the United States.

Sec. 8. There shall a court established in each county in the Nation. to be called County Courts, which shall have jurisdiction in all matters relating to disbursement of money for County and District purposes, and in every other case that may be necessary to the internal improvement and local concerns of their respective counties.

They shall have exclusive original jurisdiction in all matters of contract or controversy, except in action of covenant where the same is fifty dollars and over.

Sec. 9. The Judges of the County Courts shall in no case have jurisdiction to try and determine any criminal case or penal offence against the Nation, but may sit as examining Courts and commit, discharge or recognize to the Court having jurisdiction, for further trial of offenders against the peace, for the foregoing purposes; they shall have power to issue all necessary process: they shall have power to bind to keep the peace or for the good behavior. The presiding Judges of the County Courts shall receive for their services such compensation and fees as General Council may from time to time, by law, direct.

Sec. 10 No Judge shall preside on the trial of any cause in the event of which he may be interested, or where either of the parties shall be connected with him by affirmaty or consanguinity. within such degrees as may be prescribed by law, or in which he may have been of council, or have presided in any County Court, except by consent of all the parties. In case all or any of the Judges of the Supreme Courts, shall be thus disqualfied from presiding on any cause or causes, the Court or Judges thereof shall certify the same to the Chiefs of the Nation, who shall immediately commission, especially, the requisite number of men of law knowledge, for the trial and determination thereof. The same course shall be pursued in Circuit and County Courts as prescribed in this section, for cases in the Supreme Court. The Judge of the Circuit Courts may temporarilly appoint one of the Supreme National Judges to act in his place in the event of his inability to attend the Courti in his Circuit himself. Judges shall not charge juries with regard to maatter of fact, but may state the testimony and declare the law.

Sec. 11. There shall be a District Attorney elected in each District by the qualified electors of their respective Districts, whose compensation and terms of service shall be prescribed by law.

Sec. 12. The General Council shall have the power, by law, to prescribe the mode and manner of holding and determining suits in the Circuit and County Courts, and the manner of granting appeals.

Sec. 13. The qualified voters residing in each county elect their respective Judges to hold their office for the term of two years, and to reside in the county for which they were elected, during their continunace in the cffice.

Sec. 14. The County Judges shall, in addition to their duties that may be required of them by law, as County Judges, be Judge of the Court of Probate, and have such jurisdiction in matters relative to the estate of deceased persons, executors, adminitrators, and guardians, as may be prescribed by law, until otherwise directed by the General Council.

Sec. 15. All suits at law, or in equity, now pending in the several Courts of this Nation may be transferred to such Courts as may have proper jurisdiction thereof.

Sec. 16. All writs and other process shall run in the name of the Choctaw Nation and bear test, and be signed by the clerks of the respective Courts from which they issue.

Indictment shall conclude; "against the peace and dignity of the Choctaw Nation."

ARTICLE VII.

General Provisiosn.

Sec. 1. The Choctaw Nation shall not, after the adoption of this Constitution, be held responsible to pay any debt or debts of individuals and no money shall ever be taken from the general annuity of the Nation to be applied to any purpose whatever, unless by special appropriations of the General Council.

SEC. 2. The citizens of any of the district of the Choctaw Nation shall be entitled to all the privileges and immunities of citizenship in the several districts.

SEC. 3, The General Council shall have power by law to specify the manner in which offenders agaisnt the laws of this Nation, who may escape into the United States, or in other Indian Nations, or from one district to another in this Nation, shall be demanded, apprehended and arraigned for trial, in the several courts of this Nation having original jurisdiction thereof.

SEC. 4. Every free male citizen of this Nation, who shall have attained to the age of eighteen years, and who shall have been a citizen of this Nation six months, shall be deemed a qualified elector, and be entitled to vote in the county or district where he may actually reside at least one month preceeding the election, for each and every office made elective in this nation.

SEC. 5. All general elections shall be by ballot, and shall be commenced and be holden every year on the first Wednesday in August, and the electors, in all cases, except in cases of treason, felony and breach of the peace, shall be privileged from arrest during their attendance on elections, and on going to and returning therefrom.

SEC. 6. The General Council shall have the power, by law, to establish one or more precincts in each county in the several districtis of this Nation, and prescribed the mode and manner of holding and conducting elections, and to ascertain the number of votes polled at each precinct.

SEC. 7. The General Council shall have the power to pass such laws for raising a revenue for the support of schools in this Nation, as they may deem expedient, but for no other purpose.

SEC. 8. The oaths of office may be administered by any Judge until the General Council shall otherwise direct.

SEC. 9. The light-horsemen in this Nation shall be appointed by the Chiefs in their respective districts. There shall be one or more appointed for each county, whose duties and compensation shall be specified by law.

SEC. 10. The General Council shall have the power to pass such laws and measures as they shall deem expedient for rhe general good, provided no law be passed or adopted, contrary, to the provrsions of this Constitution.

SEC. 11. From and after the adoption of this Constitution, no free negro, or any part negro, unconnected with the Choctaw or Chickasaw blood, shall be permitted to come and settle in the Choctaw Nation.

SEC. 12. The mode of declaring war in this Nation shall be by at least two-thirds of the members of General Council, in full Council, with the approval of the Chiefs, unless in the case of actual invasion by an enemy, in which case the people shall have the right to defend themselves until the Council is convened.

SEC. 13. When a person shall be elected a member to the General Council, his term of service shall not expire until next election day.

SEC. 14. The Chiefs shall have the power, by the advice and consent of the General Council, to appoint commissioners or delegates to transact such business as may become expedient to the Choctaw Nation, and all other officers whose appointments are not herein or otherwise provided for.

SEC. 15. The General Council of the Choctaw Nation shall have the power to pass such laws as they may think expedient to punish rebelion, treason and other high crimes against the Nation.

SEC. 16. No person who is any part negro shall ever be allowed to hold any office under this Government.

SEC. 17. The General Council shall have the power, by law, to naturalize and adopt as citizens of this Nation, any Indian or descendent of an Indian—except a negro or descendent of a negro—but who on petition to the General Council, giving satisfactory proof of good character, the Council may permit them to live in the Nation

SEC. 18 All contested elections shall be determined by the General Council.

SEC. 19. Members of the General Council and all officers both Executive and Judicial shall be bound by an oath or affirmation to support the Constitution of this Nation and to perform the duties of their respective offices with faithfulness and fidelity.

Sec. 20. The Captains of the several districts shall hold their office until the expiration of the annuity under the treaty of Dancing Rabbit creek, at which time the system of captaincy as heretofore existed in the Nation shall be discontinued.

Sec. 21. Eighteen thousand dollars of the interest money arising from Chickasaw funds, granted to the Choctaws by Convention held and concluded at Doaksville, shall, after the year 1842, be set apart annually for educational purposes and the remaining seven thousand dollars shall be set apart annually to be expended for blacksmith shops and other national purposes.

Sec. 22. The General Council shall have power to create, by law, such regulations and commissions, and appoint superintendents and such other officers as the case may require for the promotion and advancement of all the schools in the Nation.

Sec. 23. Any citizen of this Nation who may find any mine or mines or mineral waters shall have exclusive right and privilege, so long as he may choose to work the same within one mile in any direction from his work or improvement, provided, however, he does not interfere with the rights of the former settler.

Sec. 24. No person who denies the being of God, or in future rewards and punishments shall hold any office in the civil department of this Nation, nor be allowed his oath in any court of justice.

Sec. 25. The Treasurer of this Nation, together with all other persons who may be entrusted with public money, shall be required to give such bond and security as may be prescribed by law.

Militia.

Sec. 26. The General Council shall have power, by law, for organizing and disciplining the militia of this Nation, in such manner as they shall deem expedient, not incompatible with the Constitution, treaties and laws of the United States, in relation thereto..

Sec. 27. The Chiefs shall have power to call forth the militia to execute the laws of the Nation, to suppress insurrection and repell invasion.

Sec. 28. The General Council shall have power, by law, to determine the compensation and fees of all officers not otherwise provided for by this Constitution.

Sec. 29. The General Council shall have the power, by law, to prescribe the mode and manner of punishing capital crimes and offenders against the laws, dignity and peace of the Nation.

Sec 30. Whenever two-thirds of the members of the General Council assembled, shall deem it necessary. they shall propose amendments to this Constitution, and if four-fifths of the next General Council, approve of such amendment, it shall become incorporated into this Constitution.

We do declare and ordain, that all the provisions in the Constitution adopted in the year 1842, and not revised nor adopted by the Convention of 1850, are hereby null and void; and that any law which may be passed contrary to the provisions of this Constitution, shall be null and void, and all right and powers not herein granted or expressed, shall be reserved unto the people.

(Signed) P. P. PITCHLYNN,
Pres. of the Convention.

George Hudson
James Garland,

Wallis Laflore,
Thomas Pitchlynn.

LAWS.

[Repealed laws are omitted; and amended laws are printed as amended.]

SESSION I.—1834.

AN ACT Preventing the introduction of whiskey.

SEC 1. *Be it enacted by the General Council of the Choctaw Nation assembled*, That no person or persons shall be permitted to bring any whiskey or other ardent spirits into this Nation; and any person so offending shall have the whiskey or other ardent spirits destroyed by the light-horse-men or any one of them; and the captains and their warriors of the several districts shall have the power, and be bound to exercise the duties of the light-horse-men in assisting to destroy any whiskey or other ardent spirits which may be brought into the Nation.

And be it further enacted, That should any person or persons refuse to have his or her whiskey or other ardent spirits destroyed by taking up arms, and should any one of the light-horse-men, captains or warriors, in self-defence, kill or destroy the life of the person or persons having whiskey or other ardent spirits, he shall be protected by the laws of this Nation. But should any offender kill or destroy the life of any person or persons who are engaged in assisting to destroy the whiskey or other ardent spirits, such shall suffer death; but should the offender only destroy or injure the property or limbs of any of the light-horse-men, captains or warriors, he or she shall be liable to a fine or punishment according to the crime.

Approved October, 1834.

By JOSEPH KINCAID,
THOMAS LEFLORE,
NITAKACHE
Chiefs.

AN ACT for punishing theft.

SEC. 2. *Be it enacted, &c.*, That any person or persons who shall take or steal any property, goods or chattels, shall return said property, goods or chattels so stolen or pay the value thereof, and shall receive such corporal punishment as may be adequate to the theft, to be determined by twelve jurors; *Provided*, That no one shall receive at any time more than thirty-nine lashes on the bare back.

Approved October, 1834.

AN ACT making the killing a person for a witch a capital offence.

SEC. 3. *Be it enacted &c.*, That any person or persons who shall kill another for a witch or wizard shall suffer death. And any person who shall publicly state that he himself or she herself is a witch or wizard, or shall say that such a person or persons are witches or wizards, and he or she knows it to be so, shall receive sixty lashes on the bare back.

Approved November 6, 1834.

AN ACT respecting Wills.

SEC. 4. *Be it enacted &c.*, That all Wills made either verbally or in writing in the presence of two or more witnesses shall be valid to all intents and purposes.

Approved November, 1834.

AN ACT for punishing infanticide.

SEC. 5. *Be it enacted, &c.*, That any person or persons who shall be convicted of the crime of infanticide shall receive sixty lashes on the bare back

Approved November 7, 1834.

AN ACT forbidding compensation and making the person destroying the stock of another, where the fence is not lawful, liable to make restitution.

SEC. 6. *Be it enacted, &c.*, That no person or persons shall be allowed any compensation for any damage that he may sustain from stock breaking into his farm, unless his or her fence be made of good rails and ten rails high.

And be it further enacted, That if any one not having a

lawful fence should destroy or injure the stock of another for breaking into his or her farm, he or she shall be liable to pay the value of the stock so injured or destroyed.

Approved November, 1834.

AN ACT pointing out the duty of the light-horse-men to visit every neighborhood twice a year.

SEC 7. *Be it enacted, &c.*, That the light-horse-men of the several districts of the Choctaw Nation shall hereafter be required to visit all the neighborhoods within their respective districts at least twice in every year, and to advise the people to abstain from spirituous liquors, and to keep good order in their neighborhoods.

Approved November 8, 1834.

SESSION II.—1835.

AN ACT defining what constitutes lawful matrimony.

SEC. 1. *Be it enacted, &c.*, That the following mode of matrimony shall be lawful in this Nation: viz. the parties shall go before any captain or preacher of the gospel in the Nation, who shall ask the groom: "Are you willing to marry this woman whom you hold by the hand as your lawful wife?" if he says, yes, then the captain or the preacher of the gospel shall then ask the woman, "Are you willing to become the wife of this man who holds you by the hand?" if she says, yes, or be silent, he shall say, "I pronounce you man and wife." *Provided*, All marriages previous to this act shall be valid and lawful, and all property shall upon the death of the husband descend to the wife and children of the deceased husband, and in case of the death of the wife the husband shall inherit the state.

Approved October 8, 1835.

SESSION 111.—1836.

AN ACT making the owners of hogs respodsible for all damages where the fence is lawful.

SEC. 1. *Be it enacted, &c.*, That a fence of four inch cracks between each rail, for two and a half feet from the ground, shall be considered a lawful fence; and hogs breaking into a field having such a fence, the owner or owners of such hogs shall be responsible for all the damages sustained, and the Courts of the several districts shall have cognizance of such cases.

Approved October, 1836.

AN ACT prohibiting the teaching of slaves to read, write or sing without the consent of the owner.

SEC. 2 *Be it enacted, &c.*, That from and after the passage of this act, if any citizen of the United States, acting as a missionary or a preacher or whatever his occupation may be, is found to take an active part in favoring the principles and notions of the most fatal and destructive doctrines of abolitionism, he shall be compelled to leave the Nation and forever stay out of it.

And be it further enacted, That teaching slaves how to read, to write or sing in meeting-houses or schools or in any open place, without the consent of the owner, or allowing them to sit at table with him shall be sufficient ground to convict persons of favoring the principles and notions of abolitionism.

Approved October 5, 1836.

AN ACT making the person who sets the woods on fire responsible for all damages done.

SEC. 3. *Be it enacted, &c.*, That if any person should be found setting the woods on fire, and if the fire should destroy any stock, fencvs or other articles of any person, and if the person or persons so injured shall be able to prove the fact against the offender, and inform the Court the said Court shall decided on the case, and shall make allowance accord- to the value of said property, and cause the same to be paid by the offender to the person or persons so injured.

Approved October 5, 1836.

AN ACT prohibiting slaves from having property or arms, and making the owners amenable therefor.

tion that he or they shall remove the obstruction or make another road around said obstruction equally as good as the former; but should any other person or persons open such obstruction, he or they shall receive the fine.

SEC. 4. *Be it enacted, &c.,* That after two months from the passage of this act, that no negro slave shall be in possession of any property or arms. And slave so offending shall forfeit all such property or arms as may be found in their possession, and said property shall be sold to the highest bidder by any of the light-horse-men, and the proceeds thereof be place in the Choctaw funds.

Be it further enacted, That any master or mistress who shall protect slaves so offending shall be liable to pay ten dollars fine for each offence.

And be it further enacted, That any nogro slaves infringing on any of the Choctaw rights shall be driven ou. of company to behave himself; and if such offender should return and intrude any further, he shall receive ten lashes by the light-horse-men or any other person.

And be it further enacted, That any good honest slaves shall be permitted to carry a gun by having a writting pass from his master or mistress.

Approved October, 1836.

—

AN ACT allowing the Choctaws to intermarry without any regard to distinction as to *Iksa.*

SEC. 5 *Be it enacted, &c.,* That the custom of not intermarrying with their own Iksa among the Choctaw people shall forever be abolished; and all persons without any distinction of Iksa are left to make their own choice as to whom they shall marry.

Approved October 6, 1836.

—

AN ACT prohibiting the obstructing or shutting up of public roads.

SEC. 6. *Be it enacted &c.,* That if any person or persons shall stop or obstuct any public roads in any way whatever, either by throwing tress across them or by making fields over them, he or they shall pay a fine not exceeding one dollar, to be determined by the Court; except on condi-

Approved October, 1836.

—

AN ACT requiring white men who wish to work in the Nation to obtain to a written permit from the Cheif or the

Agent; and so rendering any one hiring a whiteman without such permit liable for any depredation that such whiteman may commit.

SEC. 7. *Be it enacted &c*, That all white citizens of the United States, wishing to remain in the Nation under employ of any person, citizen of the Choctaw Nation, may do so by procuring permission in writing from the Chief or United States Agent. But should any person, citizen of this Nation, receive any white man into his employ, not having the regular permission to remain in the Nation, and should such white man commit any depredation, or run away with any property belonging to the Nation, the person so employing shall pay all damages, and make good to the person or persons for property so stolen or injury sustained.

Approved October 8, 1836.

AN ACT requiring property stolen from citizens of the United State, or other tribes, to be returned.

SEC. 8. *Be it enacted, &c.*, That any property, of whatsoever nature it may be, stolen by any citizen of the Choctaw Nation, from any of the neighboring tribes of Indians or citizens of the United States, and brought into the Nation, said property shall be delivered to the District Chiefs, who shall inform the United States Agent of such offenders, and the property thus stolen shall be returned if possible to the proper owner or owners.

Approved October, 1836.

AN ACT establishing the salary of the District Clerks.

SEC. 9. *Be it enacted, &c.*, That the salary of each District Clerk be fifty dollars, per annum.

Approved October, 1836.

AN ACT preventing any Indian, not a Choctaw, to settle in the Nation without permission from the General Council.

SEC. 10. *Be it enacted, &c.*, That from and after the passage of this act no person belonging to any tribe of, Indians or people, not a descendant of the Choctaws, shall be permitted to settle in the Nation, or purchase any improvement of any citizen or citizens of this Nation, unless by permission from the General Council.

Approved October, 1836.

SESSION IV.—1837.

AN ACT for punishing the abusing or disfiguring of a horse running at large.

Sec. 1. *Be it enacted &c.*, That any person taking up a horse out of the woods, knowing at the same time that the horse is not an estray, and abusing it by ill usage and disfiguring it by shaving its tail and mane, shall pay a fine not exceeding ten dollars, where the charges can be proved against him. In all such cases the courts shall determine the penalty.

Approved October 4, 1837.

—

AN ACT respecting the pay of Indian doctors.

Sec. 2. *Be it enacted &c.*, That no "sucking" or "conjuring" Indian doctor shall have the right to take any such property as horses, cattle, hogs or guns from any sick person who shall die under his care; nor from any person else unless he raises up the sick, then he shall be entitled to whatever shall be offered him; yet he shall have a right to take goods.

Approved October, 1837.

—

AN ACT making the money arising from the sales of strays to be District funds.

Sec. 3. *Be it enacted, &c.*, That all the money arising from the sales of strays shall be as District funds, and each District shall be entitled to the money raised from the strays in said District.

Approved October, 1837.

—

AN ACT laying a fine on those who sell whiskey, and also for the disposal of said fine.

Sec. 4. *Be it enacted, &c.*, That auy person who shall bring whiskey into this Nation and shall sell to any person, shall pay such fine as the court shall determine; and the informer shall receive such pay ont of the fine as the court shall adjudge; and the remaining sum shall be put in care of the clerk of the district as district funds. But should the offender not be able to raise the money, any one of the light-horse-men shall take such property as the offender may have in possession, and shall sell it, and pay the fine from the proceeds thereof.

Approved October 5, 1837.

[N. B. All the laws up to this are signed by Joseph Kincaid, Thomas Leflore and Nitakache, Chiefs.]

SESSION V.—1838.

AN ACT prohibiting any Choctaw citizen from cohabiting with a slave.

SEC. 1. *Be it enacted, &c*, That from and after the passage of this act, that if any person or persons, citizens of this Nation shall tske up with a negro slave, he or she so offending shall be liable to pay a fine not less than ten dollars nor exceeding twenty-five dollars, and shall be separated.

And for the second offence of a similar nature the party shall receive not exceeding thirty-nine lashes nor less than five on the bare bark, as the Court may drtermine, and be separated.

Approved October, 1838.

BY JOHN McKINNEY,
PIERRE JUZAN,
Chiefs.
GEORGE OKCHAYA,
Speaker.

AN ACT making any one who pulls or leaves down the fence of another liable to fine.

SEC. 2. *Be it enacted, &c.*. That any person or persons who shall be convicted as the crime or misdemeanor of of pulling and leaving down any person's field or farm fence, shall be compelled to pay such a fine as the Court may estimate the damage done to the owner of the farm.

Approved October, 1838.

AN ACT providing for the separation of man and wife ceremony.

SEC. 3. *Be it enacted, &c.*, That if any person shall put away his wife or her husband without a sufficient cause shown to the Court, such person shall be compelled to pay ten dollars; which money shall be placed in the charge of the district clerks or treasurer for public purposes; but in case the parties shall separate by mutual consent, neither of them shall be liable to a fine.

AN ACT in relation to Salt Works.

Sec. 4. *Be it enacted, &c.*, That from and after the passage of this act, no person or persons shall be allowed to settle or destroy timber within half a mile of any salt works in this Nation, and all persons who shall settle within the above named distance from such salt works shall be liable to be removed by the light-horse-men of the district in which such salt works may be established, on application being made to the Chief of the same, in case the person so settled will not remove voluntaryly upon being notified of the passage of this act.

Approved October, 1838.

AN ACT defining the pay of District Speakers.

Sec. 5. *Be it enacted, &c.*, That the Speakers in Mushulitubbi, Apakshanubbi and Pushimataha Districts shall be allowed fifty dollars per annum while they shall hold their office.

Approved October, 1838.

SESSION VI.—1839.

AN ACT improvements how near.

Sec. 1. *Be it enacted, &c.*, That from and after the passage of this act, no citizen or citizens of this Nation shall be allowed to settle on improved lands within a shorter distance than four hundred and forty yards in a direct line from a former settler, without his or her consent. And any citizen so offending or violating this act shall be liable to pay a fine for damages to such an amount of money or property as a disinterested jury may determine; and such offender or offenders shall be compelled by the light-horse-men to remove out of the limits herein specified: *Provided*, Such settlement be not within an acknowledged town, place of gathering or village.

Approved October 11, 1839.

AN ACT selling of the country

SEC. 2 *Be it enacted, &c.*, That any Chief, captain or citizen of this Nation who shall sign any instrument of writing in any way conveying or making sale of any portion or the whole of the Choctaw Nation, shall be deemed a traitor and an enemy to his country, and shall suffer death.

And be it further enacted, That any white man in this Nation, who shall advise or encourage any citizen of this Nation, verbally or in writing, to consent or agree to a sale of any part or the whole of this Nation, shall be deemed a bad man, and an enemy to the Choctaw people; and on application being made to the Agent or district chief in which such offender may be found, shall be forthwith ordered out of this Nation.

Approved October 9, 1839.

[The acts of Sessions V and VI were signed by John McKinney and Pieerre Juzan, Chiefs, and George Gkchaya, Speaker.]

SESSION VII.—1840.

AN ACT property in dispute.

SEC. 1. *Be it enacted, &c.* That from and after the passage of this act, that when disputes arise between citizens of this Nation respecting the rights of property, and upon complaint being made to the chief or judges of the district in which such difficulty may exist, it shall be their duty to order the light-horse-men to seize and hold in custody such property until the court can be held and the rights of property be tried: *Provided however*, When the defendant can give good security in the presence of one or more light-horse-men for the forth-coming of such property in dispute at the ensuing court, he or she may be permitted to hold the same until the court shall decide: and in all cases where property is held in custody for trial, the party losing the suit shall pay the light-horse-men for their services as may be determined by the court.

Approved October 7, 1840.

JAMES FLETCHER,
JOHN McKINNEY,
PIERRE JUZAN,
Chiefs.

AN ACT murderers to be arrested by order of the Chief or Judge.

SEC. 2. *Be it enacted, &c*, That all murderers and criminals in this Nation shall, by order of the chief or judge, be apprehended by the light-horse-men and held in confinement until they can be tried in the courts.

Approved October, 1840.

AN ACT making the pistols of the light-horse-men the property of the Nation.

SEC. 3. *Be it enacted &c.* That the pistols given to the Nation by the United States Government, for the use of the light-horse-men, be considered as public property, and in case of death or resignation the pistols shall be transferred to their successors in office.

AN ACT white men marrying in the Nation.

SEC. 4. *Be it enacted, &c.*, That no white man shall be allowed to marry in this Nation unless he has been a citizen of the same for two years.

And be it further enacted, That he shall be required to procure a license from some judge or the district clerk and be lawfully married by a minister of the gospel, or some other authorized person, before he shall be entitled and admitted to the privilege of citizenship.

And be it further enacted, Should any officer or minister of the gospel, who are authorized by law to marry in this Nation, perform such marriage ceremony not agreeable to this act, shall be made to pay a fine of one hundred dollars for each offence, and the money shall be put into the district treasury in which said marriage ceremony may have taken place.

And be it further enacted, That no white man who shall marry a Choctaw woman shall have the disposal of her property without her consent; and any white man parting from his wife, without just provocation, shall forfeit and pay over to his wife such sum or sums as may be adjudged to her by the district court for said breach of the marriage contract, and be deprived of citizenship.

Approved October, 1840.

AN ACT clerks and judges to keep record of the courts

TEC. 5. *Be it enacted, &c.*, That from and after the passage of this act, each clerk of the several districts shall be furnished with a large blank book out of the district funds to keep a correct record of all the proceedings of the several courts in his own district.

And be it further enacted, That the judges in the several districts of each court shall furnish the district clerk in their respective districts with a full copy of all trials under his jurisdiction, with his name signed to it, which bill shall be filed and put on record.

Approved October, 1840.

AN ACT incendiaries, destroyers of property and also of accessories.

SEC. 6. *Be it enacted, &c.*, That any person or persons who shall be convicted of the crime of burning another person's house or houses, or in any manner destroying the property belonging to a citizen of this Nation shall be subject to a fine equal to the value of the property so destroyed, and in addition, shall receive such corporeal punishment as the court may determine; but such punishment shall not exceed thirty-nine lashes on the bare back, unless such person be unable to pay the fine, in which case he, she or they shall receive one hundred lashes.

And be it further enacted, That accessories and advisors to such crime shall suffer half the burthen of the fine and punishment.

Approved October, 1840.

AN ACT runaway negroes.

SEC. 7. *Be it enacted, &c.*, That from and after the passage of this act, that it shall be the duty of any one in this

Nation to take up a negro whom he may suspect as a runaway: *Provided, however,* That any person or persons who may apprehend a negro as a runaway, he shall give the owner, where he is known, information by the earliest opportunity. And if such negro be caught any distance less than twenty-five miles from home, the person so apprehending shall be entitled to five dollars; and if caught over that distance he shall receive ten dollars from the owner of said runaway negro.

And be it further enacted, &c., That it shall be the duty of the person so taking up a runaway negro to report to the district clerk of the district in which such runaway may be taken up. And it shall be the duty of the district clerk to record the description of said runaway on his book, and for every such service the clerk shall receive five dollars, and the person who may have apprehended and secured such runaway shall be entitled to one dollar and a half per day, for every day he may have him in custody.

And be it further enacted, That it shall be the duty of the clerk to advertise the same in one or more public places in each district in this Nation. And where it appears that such runaway is from any of the United States, it shall be the duty of the clerk to send an advertisement for publication to some newspaper editor in such State.

And be it further enacted, That if no owner appears in six months after the apprehension of said runaway negro, it shall be the duty of the light-horse-men to expose such runaway or runaways to public sale. And it shall be the duty of the captain of the light-horse-men to execute a bill of sale for such negro to the purchaser. And the proceeds thereof shall be used to pay the expenses of apprehending, securing and advertising such runaway, and if there remain a balance of the proceeds it shall be put into the district funds for public purposes.

Approved October 8, 1840.

AN ACT mills made individual property.

Sec. 8. *Be it enacted, &c.,* That any citizen of this Nation who has furnished the materials to erect a mill shall be entitled to the exclusive privilege and right thereof, when completed, as his private property.

Approved October 9, 1840.

[The acts of Session VII were signed by James Fletcher, John McKinney and Pierre Juzan, Chiefs.]

SESSION VIII.—1841.

AN ACT Slander.

Sec. 1 *Be it enacted, &c.*, That any person or persons who shall slander or attempt to injure another's character shall be subject to a fine, and if unable to pay a fine, the offender shall receive such corporeal punishment as may be determined by twelve jurors, and the fine so paid shall go to the person or persons whose character has been injured.

Approved October, 1851.

JAMES FLETCHER,
JOHN McKINNEY,
ISAAC FOLSOM,
Chiefs.

AN ACT false swearing.

Sec. 2 *Be it enacted, &c.*, That if any person or persons be convicted of false swearing, or making false statements in a court of justice, such offenders shall be fined not less than ten dollars nor exceeding one hundred dollars, and shall receive not less than five nor exceeding thirty-nine lashes on the bare back.

Approved October, 1841.

AN ACT permitting Mrs. Ward and family and John and William Cooper to remain in the Nation.

Sec. 3. *Be it enacted, &c.*, That Mrs. Ward and family and William Cooper and John Cooper are hereby permitted to remain in the Nation during good behaviour.

Approved October, 1841.

[The acts of Session VIII were signed by James Fletcher, John McKinney and Isaac Folsom, Chiefs.]

SESSION IX.—1842.

AN ACT public Schools.

SEC. 1. *Be it enacted, &c.*, That there shall be, and there are hereby established the following Institutions of learning: viz. Spencer Academy, Fort Coffee Academy, Koonsha Female Seminary, Janubbi Female Seminary, Chuwahla Female Seminary and Wheelock Female Seminary.

SEC. 2. The foregoing Institutions of learning shall be, and they are hereby located at the following places: viz.

The Spencer Academy at the point on the Military Road where the buildings are erecting under the direction of the Committee appointed in 1841, about nine miles north of Doaksville. The Male branch of Fort Coffee at Fort Coffee, in Moshulatubbee District. The Female branch of this Academy shall be located in the same vicinity, by a committee who shall be appointed by the General Council for that purpose.* The Koonsha Female Seminary at such point in Pushimataha District as may be selected by a committee who shall be appointed by the General Council for that purpose. The Chuwahla and Janubbee Female Seminaries at such points in Apukshunnubbee District as may be selected by a committee who shall be appointed by the General Council for that purpose. The Wheelock Female Seminary in Apuckshanubbee District, at Wheelock.

SEC. 3. There shall be, and there is hereby appropriated the following sums for the annual support of these institutions respectively: To the Spencer Aacdemy, the sum of six thousand dollars per annum, secured to the Nation for educational purposes under the treaty made at washington City in 1825. To the Koonsha Female Seminary, three thousand dollars per annum, from the interests arising from the Chickasaw funds, agreeable to the treaty concluded at Doaksville in January, 1837. To the Wheelock Female Seminary, sixteen hundred dollars, per annum, from the same fund. To the Janubbi Female Seminary, sixteen hundred dollars, per annum, from the same fund. To the Chuwahla Eemale Seminary, sixteen hundred dollars, per annum, from the same fund. To the Fort Coffee Academy, six thousand dollars, per annum, from the same fund.

The above sums of money shall be paid over to the Superintendents of the several institutions, from time to time, as it is received from the United States. And the additional sum of three thousand dollars out of the money arising from

---

*The Female branch of this Academy is called New Hope, at the old school-house where Mr. Wilson formerly taught school about one mile from the Choctaw Agency.

the sale of the fifty four sections of land set apart in the treaty of 1820 for educational purposes, shall with the consent of the United States be applied to the support of the Koonsha Female Seminary.

SEC. 4. There is granted to each institution mentioned in this act the use of as much land as may be needed for cultivation. pasturage, &c. And also the right to take from the public domain any timber, rock, stone coal, or other materials which may be required for the use of the institution or establishment.

SEC. 5. The Superintendents and Teachers in the several institutions, with their families, if they have any, shall be furnished house room and lodging, and shall board at the same table with the pupils; but shall not receive in addition thereto, on an average, a salary more than four hundred dollars. per annum, each.

SEC. 6. Instruction in Agriculture and the Mechanical Arts shall, in the Male schools, be combined with the instruction in Letters; and in the Female Schools, in addition to Letters the pupils shall be instructed in Housewifery and Sewing, &c.

SEC 7. One tenth of all the pupils taught in these different schools shall be orphans: *Provided*, so many apply for admission.

SEC. 8 The Fort Coffee Academy under the conditions, limitations and restrictions rendered in this act, shall be placed under the direction and management of the Missionary Society of the Methodist Episcopal Church: *Provided*, said Society will contribute one thousand dollars, per annum, to the above named institution.

SEC. 9 The Koonsha Female Seminary and the Chuwahla Female Seminary. the Jamubbee Female Seminary and the Wheelock Female Seminary, under the conditions, limitations and restrictians rendered in this act, shall be placed under the direction and management of the American Board of Commissioners for Foreign Missions: *Provided*, They will contribute, annually to the above named institutions in proportion as the Methodist Episcopal Church is required to do.

Approved November, 1842.

JAMES FLETCHER,
ISAAC FOLSOM,
NATHANIEL FOLSOM,
Chiefs.

—

AN ACT attendence of light-horse-men at the Schools.

SEC. 2. *Be it enacted, &c.*, That there shall be a light-horse-man appointed to act at each of the public schools in this Nation, and to receive their appointments from the trustees and superintendents of the schools to which they shall respectively belong, and receive a salary, to be determined by the trustees and superintendents, and paid out of the school fund, and whose duties shall be specified by the trustees and superintendents.

Approved November, 1842.

—

AN ACT return of runaway children from the schools.

SEC. 3 *Be it enacted, &c.*, That when a student, who may have been placed in school under the school appropriation, shall leave the school without leave or permission, he shall be returned forthwith by his parents or guardians, or be brought back by the light horse.

Approved November, 1842.

—

AN ACT students incapable of learning.

SEC. 4. *Be it enacted, &c.*, That when a student, upon a fair trial of two years, is found, from mental inability, incapable to learn or improve, such pupils shall, at the request of the trustees, be removed from institution, and others selected to fill the vacancy.

Approved November, 1842.

—

AN ACT students under appropriation.

SEC. 5. *Be it enacted, &c.*, That the male students selected to fill the schools shall be from the age of ten to sixteen, and females from the age of eight to fourteen years.

And be it further enacted, That no family hereafter shall be allowed to put more than one child in public institutions of this Nation; but those that have already two children at said schools, they shall remain until they complete their education; and those that have more than two in shall be compelled to take them out immediately or pay the expenses to the institution.

Approved November, 1842.

—

AN ACT trading house not be to within three miles of any school.

SEC. 6. *Be it enacted, &c.*, That no person or persons shall be allowed to establish a store or trading house within three miles of any of the public schools.

Approved November, 1842.

—

AN ACT regulations of the public schools to be laid before the General Council

SEC. 7. *Be it enacted, &c.*, That the rules and regulations of each public school shall be laid before General Council for its approval.

Approved November, 1842.

—

AN ACT hickory and pecan trees.

SEC. 8. *Be it enacted, &c.*, That no person or persons shall cut down hickory or pecan trees for the nuts in this

Nation; and the persons so offending shall be liable to a fine of two dollars per tree, and one half of said fine shall go to the informer and the other half shall be as district funds.

Approved November, 1842.

AN ACT limiting the number light-horse-men in Pushimataha and Moshulatubbee Districts.

SEC. 9. *Be it enacted, &c.*, That from and after the passage of this act, the Chiefs in Pushimataha and Moshulatubbee Districts shall have the right to curtail the number of light-horse-men to six in their respective districts.

Approved November, 1842.

SESSION X.—1843.

AN ACT prohibiting the riding of a stray horse out of the Nation.

SEC. 1. *Be it enacted, &c.* That from and after the passage of this act, no man shall ever be allowed to take or ride any stray horse beyond the limits of the Choctaw Nation; and any one so offending shall pay the value thereof to the Nation or to the owner of said stray if said stray, should be lost in any way, or should be taken from him by fraud.

Approved October, 1843.

JAMES FLETCHER.
ISAAC FOLSOM.

Chiefs.

AN ACT for the punishment of assault and battery.

SEC. 2. *Be it enacted, &c.*, That from and after the passage of this act, if any person or persons should strike or otherwise injure another person without provocation, through malice, so that such injured person should lose any time from his business, the person so offending shall be liable to be sued in the courts of this Nation, and shall be subject to fine and be compelled to pay by the light-horse-men such fine as the jury may determine, which fine when collected shall be paid over to the person so maimed or injured.

Approved October, 1843.

AN ACT to prevent the harboring of runaway negroes.

SEC. 3. *Be it enacted, &c.*, That any person who shall be guilty of harboring a runaway negro or negroes, shall, upon conviction, be made to pay the owner in any sum as the case may be determined by any court having jurisdiction of the same.

Approved October, 1813.

AN ACT providing for the payment of fines.

SEC. 4. *Be it enacted, &c.*, That from and after the passage of this act, that the Judges of the several districts of the Nation, shall have power to order light-horse-men to collect all fines that may be imposed by any court of this Nation according to law; *Provided* he or she is not able to pay at the time, they shall have three months; then if not paid in that time, the Judge shall order the light-horse-men to seize on their property and sell it to the highest bidder to pay said fine.

Approved October, 1843.

AN ACT relating to all strays.

SEC. 5. *Be it enacted, &c.*, That from and after the passage of this act, that all stray property, the owner of which not known, shall be taken and posted as follows: That when any person shall take up any stray horse or horses, he shall be required to give public notice; and if the owner of such stray does not appear within three months from the time that such beast was taken up, then the one that took up shall take such stray before any judge; then it shall be the duty of the judge to authorize two or more persons to appraise the same, and the description and value taken down and writing, and a copy of the description and valuation shall be furnished the district clerk; then it shall be the duty of the district clerk to have the same advertised in one or more public places in his own district. And if the owner of such beast do not appear within twelve months, after which time the property shall be sold to the highest bidder by any light-horse-man, by first giving fifteen days notice of the sale; and one half of the proceeds shall go to the one that took up, then he shall pay the district clerk one dollar and half, and the other half of the proceeds shall go to the district in which such stray may be sold; but should the owner appear before the expiration of twelve months, and prove his or her property before any judge; he or she shall be entitled to the same by paying one dollar and a half each to the district clerk and the one that took up.

2. That every person who shall take up stray cattle shall be required to give public notice of the same, and if the owner of which do not appear within six months from the time that such stray was taken up, then the one that took up shall notify any judge of such stray property; then it shall be the duty of the judge to authorize two or more persons to appraise the same: and aslo state the age, brand, mark and color in writing, and a copy of the same shall be furnished the district clerk; then it shall be the duty of the district clerk to advertise the same in one or more public places in his district, and if the owner of such animal do not appear within twelve months, after which time the property shall be sold to the highest bidder by any light-horse-man by first giving fifteen days notice of the sale, and one half of the proceeds shall go to the one that took up; then he shall pay the district clerk one dollar per head, and the other half of the proceeds shall go to the district in which such sale may take place: but if the owner of such animal appear before the expiration of twelve months, and prove his or her property before any judge, he or she shall be entitled to the same, by paying twenty-five cents per head each to the district clerk and the one that took up.

3. That every person who shall take up stray hogs or sheep shall be required to give public notice of such strays, and if the owner of said stray does not appear within six months from the time such stray property was taken up, then the one that took up shall notify any judge of such stray property, then it shall be the duty of the judge to authorize two or more persons to appraise the same and state color and ear mark of each stray in writing, and a copy of

the same shall be furnished the district clerk, and whose duty it shall be advertise the same in one or more pulic places in his own district. And if the owner of such property should not appear within twelve months, after which time the property shall be sold to the highest bidder by any one of the light horse-men by first giving fifteen days notice of the sale, and one half of the proceeds shall go to the one that took up, then he shall pay the district clerk twenty-five cents per head; but should the owner appear before the expiration of the twelve months and prove his or her property before any judge, he or she shall be entitled to the same by paying twelve and a half cents per head each to the district clerk and the one that took up.

4. That no person shall take up any stray unless the same be found on his or her plantation, or running with his or her stock.

5. That every person shall take up a stray horse or horses shall be required to take said strays to the stray pen at every Supreme Court in their respective district and keep them during the collection of the people.

6. That every person who shall take up any stray animal, and abuse the said animal so as to cause its death, shall pay the value of the stray to the owner or to the district, as may be determined by any court having jurisdiction thereof.

7. That every person who shall take up any stray animal should fail to take said stray to the stray pen the second time, any judge shall appoint some other person or persons to take charge of said stray.

Approved October, 1843.

AN ACT stray pen.

Sec. 6. *Be it enacted, &c.*, That there shall be a stray pen of four hundred rails and good bars made in each of the three districts, at their respective Supreme Court Grounds.—Any person shall have the liberty of making the said pen, who shall be paid five dollars out of the funds arising from the sales of strays.

Approved October, 1843.

AN ACT blank books for the District Clerks.

Sec. 7. *Be it enacted, &c.*, That each clerk shall be furnished a good blank book proper for recording and stray property in their respective districts.

Approved October, 1843.

—

AN ACT duties of Treasurers and Auditors.

Sec. 8. *Be it enacted, &c.*, That from and after the passage of this act, that it shall be the duty of the District Treasurer to receive and pay over all public funds on a warrant issued from the Auditor of the public accounts in their respective districts; and whose duty it shall be to keep a strict account of all monies received and the expenditure of the same, and make a full report annually to the Gsneral Council.

And be it further enacted, That the auditor of the public accounts shall not be allowed to issue his warrant in favor or against the treasurer only in consequence of an appropriation made by the General Council.

And be it further enacted, That it shall be the duty of the auditor of the public accounts to keep a strict account of all monies paid over to the treasurer, and the amount drawn from the treasury.

And be it further enacted, That in case of death, resignation or inability of the treasurer or auditor, the Chief shall appoint another to fill the vacancy until the next General Council

And be it further enacted, That the treasurers and auditors shall each receive for their services two dollars and a half on every one hundred dollars on all money placed in their hands.

Approved October, 1843.

—

AN ACT respecting the three months shops.

Sec. 9. *Be it enacted. &c.*, That each Smith shall receive forty dollars per month, and Striker twenty dollars, and find themselves; and that said shops be under the control of the Chiefs of their respective districts.

And be it further enacted, That there shall be seven hundred pounds of iron and one hundred pounds of steel furnished to each of the district shops.

And be it further enacted, That the different district shops shall commence to work some time in March, and when they commence business they shall end in precisely three months.

And be it further enacted, That each of the district chiefs shall have the power to let out contracts for furnishing the district shop, within their respective districts, with the quantity of iron and steel and black-smith tools as stipulated in the act authorising said shops; and that such contracts will be let out to the lowest bidder. The person or persons taking such contracts will be required to give a bond and approved security for the faithful performance of such contracts, and such bonds shall be equal to the value of said contract.

Approved October, 1843.

AN ACT establishing Armstrong Academy.

Sec. 10. *Be it enacted, &c.*, That the sum of twenty-nine hundred dollars out of the four thousand and two hundred dollars be set apart and annually appropriated to be expended under the direction of the American Indian Association, in Pushimataha District, to be called Armstrong Academy; *Provided*, said American Indian Association will contribute and furnish one thousand dollars annually for the support of said Institution.

Approved October, 1843.

Sec. 11. *Be it enacted by the General Council of the Choctaw Nation assembled*, That three hundred dollars be set apart and annually appropriated for the support of Norwalk school; which shall be conducted by the American Board of Commissioners for Foreign Missions.

[The acts of Session X were signed by James Fletcher and Isaac Folsom Chiefs.]

SESSION XI.—1844.

AN ACT authorizing Judges to preserve order in time of Court.

Sec. 1. *Be it enacted, &c.*, That from and after the passage of this act, that the Judges of this Nation shall have, and are hereby invested with full power to keep good order and regulations at their respective courts. Any person or persons who should come and threaten the life of any person at court, or treat the court with contempt while in session, shall be taken into custody by the light-horse-men and fined not exceeding fifty dollars, the same to be determined by the judges of the court; and if the offender be unable to pay the money the judge shall have the right to order the light-horse men to take any property belonging to him, and sell it to the highest bidder, and pay the said fine. The money thus collected shall go to the district treasurer for the use of district purposes.

And be it further enacted, That any person or persons refusing to be taken into custody for any criminal offences or for contempt of court, and shall take up any unlawful weapens, the light-horse-men shall have the power to take them dead or alive, and they shall be protected by the laws of this Nation.

Approved October, 1844.

THOMAS LEFLORE,
NATHANIEL FOLSOM,
NITAKACHI,
ISAAC ALBERTSON,
Chiefs.

—

AN ACT trading with slaves.

SEC. 2. *Be it enacted, &c.*, That from and after the passage of this act, if any citizen of this Nation is known to trade or carry on trafficking of any nature whatsoever with any negro slave belonging to this Nation, and the fact can be established, said offender shall be liable to an indictment in any court or courts of this Nation having jurisdiction thereof, and shall be made to pay a fine of five dollars; and the fine when collected, one half shall go to the treasury as district funds in which such transaction may take place, and the other half shall go to the informer: *Provided, however*, any citizen wishing to trade with any negro slave in this Nation may do so by the consent of the owner or by the negro having a written permit to that effect.

Approved October 18 1844.

AN ACT Board of Ttrustees, their pay and duties.

SEC. 3. *Be it enacted, &c.*, That from and after the passage of this act, that P. P. Pitchlynn, George W. Harkins, Robert M. Jones and Thompson McKinney be and are hereby appointed Board of Trustees for all the Public Schools in this Nation, and they and their successors as Board of Ttrustees, shall each receive fifty dollars per annum for their services out of the public funds.

AN ACT Trustees to examine the account of schools.

SEC. 4. *Be it enacted, &c.*, That it shall be the duty of the Board of Trustees, collectively or separately, to examine the accounts of the Public Schools quarterly, or at such time as may be necessary, and if correct, to certify upon honor to the correctness of the same.

Approved October, 1844.

AN ACT free negroes not to have any share in the Annuity or public shops.

SEC. 5. *Be it enacted, &c.*, That no free negro, unconnected with Choctaw blood, shall ever be allowed to draw any money from the Choctaw Annuity.

And be it further enacted, That no free negro shall participate in any of the black-smith shops belonging to the Choctaw Nation.

Approved October, 1844.

AN ACT providing for the removal of some Indians in the Nation.

SEC. 6. *Be it enacted, &c.*, That all the intruding tribes, of Indians that are now residing within the limits of the Choctaw Nation, shall be required to leave the Nation as soon as practicable. And that the Chiefs of the Nation be required to inform Major William Armstrong, United States Agent, of the existence of this act, and requst him to have them removed without the limits of the Choctaw Nation: *Provided, However*, The Cadoes, who at a previous Session of the General Council having obtained a permit to live in the Nation, shall be exempt from the operation of this Act; and also the following named families of Indians be allowed the remain unmolested by the operation of this Act, viz: Charley, Mike. McCoy, Cherokees; Little Boy and Frank's family and Strong Man, Delewares; Capt. Beaver, Panther and Oats, Shawnees, and their families; and one family of Quapaws living above the mouth of Washita, on Red river.

Approved October, 1844.

[The acts of Session XI were signed by Thomas Leflore, Nitakache, Isaac Albertson and Nathaniel Folsom, Chiefs.]

SESSION XII.—1845.

AN ACT Patent from the United States.

SEC. 1. *Resolved, &c.*, That the Patent from the United States Government for the Choctaw country, shall be placed in the hands of Col. Thomas Leflore for safe keeping.

Approved October, 1845.

THOMAS LEFLORE,
NITAKACHE,
ISAAC ALBERTSON,
Chiefs.

AN ACT Spencer Academy and Norwalk school.

SEC. 2. *Be it enacted, &c.*, That Spencer Academy shall be placed under the control and direction of the Assembly's Board: *Provided*, that Board will contribute two thousand dollars annually to the support of the Institution; to be conducted in the same manner, with the same privileges, restrictions and conditions provided in the school act entitled: "An Act providing for a system of Public Instruction in the Choctaw Nation," passed 29th of November, 1842. And it shall be the duty of the School Trustees to request Rev. Cyrus Kingsbury to correspond with the above Board upon the subject, and if they will accept the terms offered, to urge them to come and take charge of the Institution at the earliest time possible.

And be it further enacted, That the salary heretofore received by Mr. Rind shall be expended upon Norwalk School, to be under the control and management of the American Board of Commissioners for Foreign Missions: *Provided*, said Board will contribute the proportion to the supprt of the

school as agreed upon in the general School Act of 1842.
Approved October 7, 1845.

AN ACT granting time to Criminals before execution
SEC. 3. *Be it enacted, &c.*, That from and after the passage of this act, that when criminals in this Nation are sentenced to death, the judge, after consulting the wishes of the criminal as to the time when he would wish to be executed, shall set the time, not exceeding ten days after the judgment is paseed, Sundays excepted. In the mean time the judge shall order the light-horse-men to keep him in close confinement till the day of execution.
Approved October 8, 1845.

AN ACT current expenses of the Chickasaw Dist.
SEC. 4. *Be it enacted, &c.*, That the General Council of the Choctaw Nation, assembled, have no right to appropriate out of their National funds to pay the current expenses of the Chickasaw District.
Approved October 9, 1845.

AN ACT Introducer or seller of whiskey liable for damages.
SEC. 5. *Be it enacted, &c.*, That from and after the passage of this act, any person or persons who shall bring spirituous liquors into this Nation, and give or sell it to any person or persons, and any person or persons thereby be maimed or injured, the one who brought and gave or sold it shall be liable to an action in court, and be made to pay a fine not less than one dollar nor exceeding one hundred dollars, and the fine so paid shall one half go to the person so maimed or injured and the other half to the district in which such suit may be brought.
Approved October 9, 1845.

AN ACT removing three months shop to Oklakintubbi's
SEC. 6. *Be it enacted, &c.*, That from and after the passage of this act, that the three months shop in Apakshanubbi District at Filihkatubbi shall be removed to a Spring near Oklakintubbi's
Approved October 9, 1845.

AN ACT contracts from the several public schools.

SEC. 7. *Be it enacted; &c.*, That from and after the passage of this act, that no contract or contracts, issued from the public institutions, shall be given to any person who is not a citizen of this Nation, when the same can be furnished by citizens of this Nation as low as can be done by citizens of the States.

And be it further enacted, That Major William Armstrong be informed of the existence of this act by the Chiefs of this Nation.

Approved October 10, 1845.

[The acts of Session XII were signed by Thomas Leflore, Nitakache and Isaac Albertson, Chiefs.]

SESSION XIII.—1846.

SEC. 1. *Be it enacted, &c.*, That if any student in the public schools in this Nation shall run off and go home with his clothes, that were given to him at the institution, and the parents or guardian of such student should or neglect to send him or his clothes back in the time prescribed, he or they shall be made to pay the value thereof from the annuity of such students, and parents or guardians.

Approved October 15, 1846.

SEC. 2. *Be it enacted, &c.*, That the Board of Trustees of public Schools in this Nation shall be elected every four years by the General Council.

Bill proposed by Jonathan Cogswell.

Approved October 15, 1846.

SEC. 3. *Be it enacted &c.*, That no negro slave can be emancipated in this Nation, except by application or petition of the owner to the General Council, and *Provided also*, that it shall be made to appear to the Council the owner or owners, at the time of application, shall have no debts outstanding against him or her, either in or out of this Nation. Then, and in that case, the General Council shall have the power to pass an act for the owner to emancipate his or her slave, which negro, after being freed, shall leave this Nation within thirty days after the passage of the act. And in case said free negro or negroes should return into this Nation afterwards, he, she or they shall be subject to be taken by the light-horse-men and exposed to public sale for the term of five years; and the funds arising from such sale shall be used as National funds.

Approved October 15, 1846.

SEC 4. *Be it enacted, &c.*, That from and after the passage of this act, no negroes from the United States, or neighborihg tribes of Indians, will be allowed to come and remain in this Nation, under the presence of hiring himself or themselves to work, no matter whether they have papers or not.

And all negroes violating the provisions of this act, shall be taken up by the light-horse-men of the District where such offender may be found, and shall receive on the bare back, not less than one hundred lashes each.

And be it further enacted That all property, goods or chattels found in his or their possession, shall be seized and sold at public sale, and one-third of the proceeds shall go to the light-horse-men and the balance thereof be applied to some beneficial purposes in the District: *Provided, however*, That the above bill shall not extend to negroes passing through the country, or such as may be hauling for citizens or merchants in this Nation.

Bill proposed by Robert Love.

Approved October 15, 1846.

SEC. 5. *Be it enacted, &c.*, That from and after the passage of this act, that any person or persons disturbing any religious devotions shall be taken up and presented before the judge by the light-horse-men, who is hereby authorized by law to fine them, but the fine shall not exceed five dollars for each person so offending, and the fine so collected shall belong to the district in which it may be collected.

Proposed by Robert Love.

Approved October 16, 1846.

SEC. 6. *Be it enacted, &c.*, That all witnesses summoned to attend court shall be allowed two cents per mile going and returning from court, and fifty cents per day whilst attending at court till discharged; to be collected by the lighthorse-men off the person losing the suit, except in cases of murder, in which case the district shall pay the witnesses, in behalf of the prosecuting party.

Approved October 16, 1846.

SEC. 7. *Be it enacted, &c.*, That all temporary Clerks at every election, in the several districts of this Nation, shall each receive one dollar per pay out of the estray funds.

Proposed by Allen Carney.

Approved October 16, 1846.

SEC. 8. *Be it enacted, &c.*, That no person shall be appointed or elected Judge in this Nation unless he can read the English or Choctaw Language.

SEC. 9. *Be it enacted, &c.*, That the law passed in Session 9th, Sec. 8, be amended so as to read thus: That when there is a charge or charges brought against any one under the employment of the different schools in this Nation, the person so accused shall have a fair and impartial trial by the Board of Trustees before he shall be removed from Institution.

By, Allen Carney.

Approved October 16, 1846.

SEC. 10. *Be it enacted, &c.*, That every person who shall be convicted of having forged, counterfeited, or falsely altered any Will. Deed of gift, Note or Order, or any other instrument in which any value consideration may be in question, shall be guilty of Forgery, and shall be punished with not less than thirty-nine lashes, and fined not less than twenty-five, nor exceeding five hundred dollars.

Bill proposed by R. M. Jones.

Approved October 16, 1846.

SEC. 11. *Be it enacted, &c.*, That any person who shall be convicted of the crime of committing rape or forcibly ravishin a woman or girl, shall receive one hundred lashes laid on his bare back. And for the second offence of the same nature the offender shall suffer death. But in case of an attempt only, to ravish a woman or girl, the court shall determine the penalty; but the guilty person shall not receive more than thirty lashes on the bare back.

Approved October 16, 1846.

Sec. 12. *Be it enacted, &c.*, That from and after the passage of this act, no person or persons shall be allowed to drive horses, mules, cattle, hogs, or sheep from the range to which the same may belong. But it shall be the duty of every person or persons who may be driving horses, mules, cattle, hogs, or sheep, if any such stocks, not belonging to his or her drove, should join the drove, he or she who may be driving, shall halt the drove at the nearest pen or some other convenient place, and separate all such stock as do not belong to his or her drove, or the person or persons for whom they may be employed to collect or drive stock.

And be it further enacted, That if any person or persons shall violate the provisions of this act, shall pay a fine and damages according to the decision of the district court where such offence may be committed, for the use and benefit of the person or persons sueing for the same.

And if any slave or slaves, employed in driving stock, should violate the foregoing provisions of this act, his or their owner or employer shall be liable to pay a fine and damages, according to the provisions of this act.

Proposed by Forbis Leflore.

Approved October 16, 1846.

Sec. 13. *Be it enacted, &c.*, That all witnesses who are summoned to attend court and cannot go in case he is sick or his family, and gives a good lawful excuse, he, she, or they will be required to give their statement under oaths before any acting judge, and the said judge shall take his or her statement in writing, which shall answer the same as if it had been made in court.

By G. W. Harkin.

Approved October 17, 1846.

Sec. 14. *Be it enacted, &c.*, That from and after the passage of this act, the District Attornies of the several districts of this Nation, shall be selected every year by the qualified electors within their respective districts, whose duties shall be to report all offences against the laws of this Nation to the judge in his district, and to prosecute them to the best of his abilities. Bill proposed by Jonathan Cogswell.

Approved October 17, 1846.

[The acts of Session XIII were signed by Thomas Leflore, S. D. Fisher, Peter Folsom and James McLaughlin Chiefs.]

SESSION XIV.—1847.

AN ACT granting rights and privileges to certain Cherokees

Sec. 1. *Be it enacted, &c.*, That by authority vested in us in the 13 Section of the general provisions in the Constitution. We do grant and extend to John, Elizabeth J. Richard Brown of the Cherokee Nation equal rights privileges immunities and franchise, held and enjoyed in the Nation by the Choctaw citizens with the exception of that forbidden in the constitution, and furthermore shall not participate in the annuities, Public Shops and schools.

Proposed by R. M. Jones.

AN ACT separating man and wife.

Sec. 2. *Be it enacted, &c.*, That from and after the passage of this act, any person who shall be found guilty of taking or separating a woman from her husband who was lawfully married he or they so offending shall pay a fine of ten dollars which shall go to the District treasnry, and the parties restored to each other if they wish it.

AN ACT District Attorneys Fees.

Sec. 3. *Be it enacted, &c.*, That from and after the passage of this act, the district Attorneys of the several districts shall be allowed in addition to their salary, one half of the fine for every case they shall prosecute on any person or persons violating the laws of the Nation out of the fine that goes to the district treasury

And be it further enacted That in case the District Attornies fail to attend, and prosecute the suit at court, the judges shall have the power to appoint any person to act in his place during the term of the court and who shall be allowed one half the fine afore said for his Services.

Proposed by Thompson Mckinney.

AN ACT Division of the permanent shop.

SEC. 4. *Be it enacted, &c.*, That the funds appropriated by the United States Government to the support of the shop now located on Sugar Loaf creek, shall be divided as follows: viz, one hundred and eighty dollars to the treasurer of Moshulatubbee District, one hundred & eighty dollars to the treasurer Pushimataha district, one hundred & eighty dollars to the treasurer of Puckshunubbee districts. And the residue of sixty dollars to the treasurer of Puckshunubbee and Pushimataha Districts for the support of three months shop in the several districts to be located by law as may be directed hereafter. And that the Iron and steel which may be furnished by the Government shall be equally divided in the three afore said districts.

Proposed by Thomas Wall.

AN ACT selecting scholars to enter College.

SEC. 5. *Be it enacted, &c.*, by the General Council of the Choctaw Nation assembled. That so soon as a male student becomes qualified to enter College, the trustees shall select and send them to some good College in the United States to obtain a classical education.

Proposed by committee schools.

AN ACT disturbing the peace of families.

SEC. 6. *Be it enacted, &c.*, That from and after the passage of this act, that if any person or persons who shall go into the inside of the enclosure or into the house of any person or persons and use abusive language and disturb the peace of any family or families shall be liable to pay a fine to be determined by court, such fine shall not exceed fifty dollars nor less than five dollars which shall go to the injured party.

AN ACT government and discipline of Spencer Academy.

SEC. 7. *Be it enacted &c.*, A communication having been received from the Secretary of the board of foreign missions of the Presbyterian church relative to the Government of Spencer Academy and the same being under consideration.

Be it further enacted, That we consider the Government control and discipline of Spencer Academy to be vested in the aforesaid Board of foreign missions with the proviso (viz.) That the board of trustees of public schools appointed by the General Council of the Choctaw Nation receive the right of investigating and reporting to the council relative to the conduct of any teacher or Superintendent against whom any serious charges may be made and the general council of the Choctaws has the power according to the ninth Section of the school law, to require the aforesaid board to remove such teacher or superintendent.

2. The trustees of the schools also reserve the right of acting with the Superintendent in cases when it may be necessary to expel pupils from any of the public schools in the Choctaw Nation.

AN ACT empowering the Chief to call upon the other chiefs to aid him.

SEC. 8. *Be it enacted, &c.*, That from and after the passage of this act, that in case the light-horse-men of any district shall not be able to execute the orders of the chief or judges of any of the several districts they shall report the same to the chief of their district who shall have the power to call upon the chief or chiefs of the other districts, to aid him with his light-horse-men in executing his orders.

By R. M. Jones.

AN ACT Appointing an additional light-horse in Pushimataha District.

SEC. 9. *Be it enacted &c.*, That there be an additional light-horse appointed in Pushimataha District to receive the same pay out of the national funds for his services.

By James McCoy.

AN ACT guardians for orphan minors.

SEC. 10. *Be it enacted, &c.*, That all orphan minors having neither father nor mother shall have a guardian appointed for them by court.

And be it further enacted, That a skedule of the property belonging to the orphan minors shall be made out by two responsible persons appointed by the judge of the county court and be placed on record in the office of the district secretary.

And be it further enacted, That before a guardian enter upon the duties of his office, shall be duly sworn by the Judge for the faithful performance of his duties and he shall be required by the court to give a fair and full statement annually of the condition of all and each kind of property placed in his hands, and the same be put on record as aforesaid so that the property may not be wasted or squandered.

And be it further enacted, And if there is any slave or slaves belonging to the estate, and which can be spared from the service which is necessary to keep for the support of the orphans, shall be hired out to the highest bidder for the benefit of said orphans.

And be it further enacted, That the guardian shall keep a strict account of all the expenses incured and the amount of wages arising from the hire of slave or slaves, and give an account of them to the district court and the same entered upon the record.

And be it further enacted, That if the means will enable the guardian he shall make every effort to give the orphan under his charge an education.

And be it further enacted, That all orphans destitute of property and who are not in the hands of relatives or friends the court shall appoint a guardian for them, whose duty shall be to look out a good home for them and bind them out where they may be kindly treated clothed and fed and trained up in the habits of industry, and where means of instruction may be given to them, if such means are convenient.

And all orphan minors having little property, shall also be placed in like manner.

And be it further enacted, That there shall be no debts collected of the estate of any deceased person until the expiration of twelve months from the day of his death. And be it further enacted, That in case of the death of an individual during intestate having a family and being possessed of an estate the court shall have the right to appoint two or three competent persons to take an account of said property assessing the value of the same and return schedule to the judge of the county court, who with the aid of said selected men or commissioners may estimate a division of said estate equally among the widow and children of the deceased person.

And be it further enacted, That the widow shall have the preference of being appointed guardian for the minor children or such person or persons as she may recommend to the court.

And be it further enacted, That all persons before they enter on their guardianship shall enter into a good and sufficient bond with approved security in a sum at least equal in value to the estate taken in charge of. And that in case of a failure of complying with such bond, the principal and securities shall be proceeded against in court, compelling the principal and securities to return the property or pay the value of the same—and the light-horse-men may be instructed by the court to make such collections.

Be it further enacted, That all minors shall be deemed competent to take charge of their estate so soon as they marry, or a male arriving at the age of twenty, and female at sixteen years.

Be it further enacted, That the guardian shall receive three per cent out of the estimate of the property that may beplaced in his or her charge.

And be it further enacted, that this act shall not be construed as to interfere with the provisions of a will.

—

AN ACT granting to new emigrants equal rights.

Sec. 11. *Be it enacted, &c.,* That all the late and new emigrant Choctaws to this country have equal rights with the old settlers in participation of all public blacksmith shops and schools in this Nation.

—

AN ACT locating the three months shops in the several

districts.

Sec. 12. *Be it enacted, &c.*, That from and after the passage of this act, the following shops shall be established, viz: in Mushalatubbe district, the shop formerly established at Thomas Wall's, be removed to the Holetasha camp-ground, and the shop at little Sam boy, be removed and established at a spring at D. Folsom's new place, and the shop at Fushmaline, be removed and located at Canady McCurtain's, and the shop on Gainsark, shall be established at Hoyubbee's.

And in Pushimataha district, that the court and 3 month's shop cite, be and the same is hereby located at Tiger spring near Armstrong Academy, and the shop formerly at Silas D. Fishers, be established at his Saw Mill, and the fourth three months shop, be located at the annuity ground, and the joint shop between Puckshinnubbee and Pushimataha districts, shall be located by a committee appointed by Col. Leflore and Fisher. And in Puckshinnubbee district, the new three months shop shall be established at standing pine. And that all shops and court ground heretofore established by law and removed by this act, are hereby repealed.

Be it further enacted, That the shop at Good Water, J. Fraziers and Bushpotuppa's in Puckshiunubbee district remain in their present location.—1847.

SESSION XV.—1848.

AN ACT officers of this nation guilty of selling whiskey or getting drunk liable to impeachment.

Sec. 1. *Be it enacted, &c.*, That from and after the passage of this act, any chiefs, captains or any other officers who were elected either by the people or the General Council, shall be found guilty of selling whiskey or any other spirituous liquor or being found drunk twice from the affects of whiskey or any other liquors, shall be liable to impeachment according to the provision made in the Constitution.

And be it further enacted, That all officers under the appointment of the chiefs, who shall be found guilty of violating the preceeding portion of this act, shall be removed from office forthwith by the chiefs of their respective districts.

And be it further enacted, That any of the chiefs who shall neglect to discharge his duty in office, as expressly specified in the above act. shall be liable to be impeached.

Approved Oct. 9 1848.

THOS. LEFLORE.
S. D. FISHER.
PETER FOLSOM.
Chiefs.

AN ACT pay of jurymen.

SEC. 2. *Be it enacted, &c.*, That from and after the passage of this act, all jurymen, when summoned to try any case in suit, shall each receive fifty cents for their fees to be paid by the person losing such suit, except in case of murder, the district shall pay the jurors out of any money unappropriated.

And be it further enacted, That the judge or judges of the court, in which such suit may be determined, shall order the light-horse-men to collect such fees either in money or property at a fair valuation and pay the same over to said jurymen. But in case the person or persons losing suit, should be unable to make immediate payment, he or she shall be indulged three month to make payment.

And be it further enacted, That so much of the section 15 session 10, which authorises 25 cents to be paid to jurymen, be and the same is hereby repealed.

Approved Oct. 9, 1848.

THOS. LEFLORE.
S. D. FISHER.
PETER FOLSOM.
Chiefs.

AN ACT stock killing one another.

SEC. 3. *Be it enacted, &c.*, That from and after the passage of this act, that all property consisting of horses, cattle jacks, jennies, mules, hogs, sheep goats and dogs, that may kill each other, the animal that was killed shall be valued by three disinterested persons, and the person whose beast was killed shall receive half the amount of his valuation from the beast that done the damage, to be collected by the light-horse-men.

Approved Oct. 9, 1848. *By the Chiefs.*

AN ACT stud jack or jackmule to be altered.

SEC. 4. *Be it enacted, &c.*, That from and after the passage of this act, that if any stud-horse, jack or jackmule is found with any persons horse or horses, and the owner be known, he shall be notified to take him away and should he refuse or neglect to do so, in due time or in case the owner of such beast or beasts be unknown, he shall be taken to the nearest person who understands castrating and have him altered, and should such a horse, jack or jackmule recover, the owner shall pay to the taker up, and the person who castrated him, one dollar each.

And be it further enacted, That should the owner refuse to pay such fine the amount may be collected by the light-horse-men who shall have one additional dollar for his trouble. But should the horse, jack or jackmule die from castration, the owner will not be required to pay any thing.

Approved Oct. 9, 1848.

THOS. LAFLORE,
S. D. FISHER,
PETER FOLSOM.
Chiefs.

AN ACT charge to juros by the judge as to the points of the law.

SEC. 5. *Be it enacted &c.*, That from and after the passage of this act, the judge of any trial shall give a charge to the jurors as to the points of the law, that is equitable to the case on trial; and Be it further enacted that the names of the jurors be put on record with the judgment and the name of the lawyers of each party.

Approved Oct. 10, 1848. *By the Chiefs.*

AN ACT summoned jurors how considered guilty of misdemeaner.

SEC. 6. *Be it enacted, &c.*, That from and after the passage of this act, if any person is summoned or sworn as a juror in any case shall take anything to give his verdict for or against any party in any case or proceeding, civil or criminal or shall receive any paper, evidence, or information from any one, in relation to any matter or cases for trial, for which he shall be summoned, he shall be deemed guilty of a misdemeanor, and on conviction shall be fined in any sum not exceeding fifty dollars, and such fine, one half shall go to the district fund, and the other half shall be equally divided between the district attorney and the light-horse who shall be at the trouble of collecting said fine.

And be it further enacted, That every judge or other persons, whose duty it shall be to select or summon any jurors in any court or before any officers who shall be guilty of any unlawful, partial or improper conduct in selecting or summoning any jurors, shall be deemed guilty of a misdemeanor, and be fined in any sum not exceeding fifty dollars, and such fine shall be collected by the light-horse-men, and one half go to the district funds and the other half shall be divided between the district attorney and the light-horse who shall be at the trouble of collecting said fine.

Approved Oct. 10, 1848. *By the Chiefs.*

—

AN ACT county judges appoint their own clerks.

Sec. 7. *Be it enacted, &c.,* That from and after the passage of this act, the inferior judges shall appoint their own clerk in their respective courts, and whose duty it shall be to keep all the proceedings and take the description of the stray at every court, and shall each receive for their service five dollars per annum, out of the district funds.

And be it further enacted, That it shall be the duty of the clerk of the court, to furnish the district clerk the description of the stray property which they may have posted at their respective courts, and shall be entitled to receive one half of the funds which goes to the district clerk, as prescribed by law, relating to estray property, passed 1843.

And be it further enacted, That the chief shall furnish for each court, paper and ink which amount is to be paid out of the district funds.

Approved Oct. 10, 1848. *By the Chiefs.*

—

AN ACT intestate or without a will.

Sec. 8. *Be it enacted. &c.,* That from and after the passage of this act, the property of all persons who die intestate or without a will, shall descend to his legal wife, or husband

and their children.

2. *And be it further enacted,* That in case such deceased person has neither wife nor husband nor children his or her grand children (if any) shall inherit the estate.

3. *Be it further enacted,* That in case there is no grand child, the father or mother of such deceased person or either of them shall heir the estate.

4. *Be it further enacted,* That in case such deceased person, has neither wife nor husband, children or grand children or father or mother, his or her estate shall go to his or her brothers, and sisters, and if none, to their lawful children.

5. Should there be none of the above mentioned relatives to the intestate deceased person, the estate shall descend to the half Brothers and sisters of the deceased person and to their legal issue.

Approved Oct. 10, 1848. *By the Chiefs.*

AN ACT married persons each to retain the right of their property

SEC. 9. *Be it enacted, &c.,* That from and after the passage of this act, when a man and women intermarry with each other, each one shall retain the right of the property that he or she may bring into the marriage union at the time they are joined together in the bonds of matrimony, and neither party shall have the right to dispose of the others property without the consent of the other.

And be it further enacted, That when the property of the wife or husband is disposed of by either party without the consent of the other, a suit may be instituted in the courts of this nation, and the property so disposed, restored or the value thereof recovered.

And be it further enacted, That no will that is made by the husband or wife, conveying property without the consent of the other shall be valid. And be it further enacted, that all property that may be accumulated by the joint exertions of a man and his wife after they are married, shall be held in common and subject to the disposal of the husband for the mutual support and benefit of the family.

And be it further enacted; That no man cupatence or verbal will, shall be valid unless the same be witnessed by two

or more disinterested witnesses.
Approved Oct. 10, 1848. *By the Chiefs.*

—

AN ACT stray property to be sold at any court except horses.
SEC. 10. *Be it enacted, &c.*, That from and after the passage of this act, all stray property which may be posted as prescribed by the act, 5th session, passed in 1843, be sold at any court, except horses, shall be sold at the supreme court, annuity, or election days, and at the General Council.
Approved Oct. 10, 1848. *By the Chiefs.*

—

AN ACT District clerk to furnish judges and Captains of the light-horse each a copy of the laws.
SEC. 11. *Be it enacted, &c.*, That the chiefs are hereby authorized to instruct the District clerks to furnish each one a copy of the laws to the judges of the superior and inferior courts as soon as practicable.
And be it further enacted That the chiefs are hereby authorize to furnish each clerk in their respective districts with paper and Ink out of the stray funds.
Approved by Thomas Leflore.
S. D. Fisher.
Peter Folsom.

Chiefs.

—

AN ACT one light-horse from each District to attend the General Council by order of the Chiefs.
SEC. 12. *Be it enacted &c.*, That from and after the passage of this act, the District chiefs shall each send one of their light-horse-men to attend the General Council at each session to act as sergent at arms.
And be it further enacted, that such light-horse-men shall receive ten dollers for their services to be paidout of the district funds in their respective district.

—

AN ACT light-horse to have the right to call upon any citizen for aid.
SEC. 13. *Be it enacted &c.*, That the light-horse-men of the several Districts shall have the right to call upon any citizen of this Nation to aid him in taking criminal charged

with high crime against this nation or destroying any whiskey, and such person who refuse to aid him in taking such criminal or destroying any whiskey unless for some lawful excuse, shall be subject to a fine not exceeding five dollars.

And one half of such fine shall go to the District fund, and the other half shall be equally divided bewteen the district Attorney, and the lighthorse-men.

AN ACT murder.

SEC. 14. *Be it enacted, &c.*, That if any person or persons shall within this nation commit the crime of wilful murder, such person or persons on being thereof convicted shall suffer death.

2. *Be it further enacted,* That any persion who shall kill a human being while in a state of Intoxication shall upon conviction thereof he adjudged guilty of wilful murder.

3. *Be it further enacted,* That any person or persons who shall administer any poison or other noxous or distructive substance or liquid with the intention to cause the death of such person shall upon conviction thereof be adjudged guilty of wilful murder,

4. *Be it further enacted,* That the manner of inflicting capital punishment in all cases hereafter shall be shot by any one of the light-horse-men.

5. *Be it further enacted* That any person who shall kill another person in self defence shall be justifiable. Though in all cases of self defence it must appear, that the danger was so urgent and pressing, that in order to save his own life or prevent his receiving great bodily injury before the mortal blow or injury was given.

6. *Be it further enacted,* That every man's house or place of residence shall be adjudged in law his castle.

7. *Be it further enacted,* That any person who shall kill another person by accident shall be excusable, as where a man is doing a lawful act, without intention of killing, or where an officer; is properly punishing a criminal and the infliction of such punishment happen to be the cause of his death.

Approved October 12. 1848.

Chiefs

SEC. 15. *Be it enacted, &c.*, That from and after the passage of this act, if any negro slave shall kill or murder another negro slave, he or she, so committing murder shall be tried in the courts of this nation, in the same manner as free citizens are tried for such offences. But in case such slave or slaves are condemned and suffer death there shall be an end to it.

And be it further enacted. That all persons who may be convicted of the crime of wilfully murdering a negro, he or she so offendi[illegible] shall suffer death in the manner provided by law, in cases of murder.

And be it further enacted, That from and after the passage of this act, that any negro slaves who shall be found at such assembles or strolling about from one plantation to another without a pass from his master mistress or overseer shall receive any number, not exeeeding ten on his or her bare back, by an[illegible] of the light-horse-men or any citizens of this nation.

Be it further enacted, That no slaves be suffered to buy or sell whiskey or other intoxicating liquors, in any way whatever such slaves so offending shall be subject to suffer any number of lashes at the discretion of the lighthorse or citizens, not exceeding thirty nine lashes on his or her bare back.

Approved Oct[illegible]ber. 12, 1848.

Thomas Leflore
Silas D. Fisher.
Peter Folsom.

—

AN ACT $555,56 an annual appropriation for neighborhood schools.

SEC 16 *Be it enact &c,*. That the sum of $555,56 be set a part and annually appropriated for the support of neighborhood and sabbath schools in Puckshunubbee district and that the sum of $222,22 cts. be set apart and annually, appropriated for the support of neighborhood and sabbath schools in each of the other two districts Moshulatubbee, and Pushimataha the cities of said schools in the several Districts to be selected and the funds appropriated under the direction of such trustees as may be appointed by the Chiefs in their respective Districts.

AN ACT working on public Roads.

SEC. 17 *Be it enacted &c.*, That from and after the passage of this act, that it shall be lawful to work on public road in this nation.

2. *Be it further enacted*, That it shall be the duty of the Captains to require the people to work on the public road six days in each year.

3 *Be it further enacted*, That it shall be the duty of the Captains to notify the people at least five days before working on the road, and any person or persons not complying to the notification shall be compelled to pay a fine not less than fifty cents per day and such fine shall be placed in the hands of the Captain to hire another person to work in his place such fine to be collected by the light-horse.

4. *Be it further enacted*, That no person will be required to work on the public road. that live over six miles from any public road.

5. *Be it further enacted*, That Docters teachrs, and students of any schools in this nation are exempt from working on the public road.

6. *Be it further enacted*, That judges of the supreme court to appoint a committee to lay out any public road in this naticn.

7. *Be it enacted*, That each warrior shall be required to birng an axe or hoe to work on the road with.

Approved October 12, 1848.

Thomas Leflore.
S. D. Fisher.
Peter Folsom.

Chiefs.

AN ACT guardian to sell the property of orphans by order of the Court.

SEC. 18. *Be it enacted &c.*, That from and after the passage of this act, that it shall be lawful for any person who may be appointed guardian for minor children to get an order from court to sell any real estate or personal property for the benefit of such minor either in or out of this nation.

and such sales shall be good and binding on such minor where they became of an age.

By R M Jones

Approved October 12, 1848.

Thomas Lebore.
S. D. Fisher.
Peter Folsom.

Chiefs.

AN ACT Granting to J. G. Ring the right to build a tall brigde.

Sec. 19. *Be it enacted, &c.* That the privilege is hereby granted John G. Ring of the Choctaw Nation the exclusive right to build a tall Bridge a cross the Poteau river at any point from the mouth to Nidever's ford on said stream.

Be it further enacted, That the said Ring shall not interfere with any right, that any citizen of this nation may have to establish ferries on said stream without their consent.

Be it further enacted That this right and privilege is granted with the understanding that the same may be renewed at the expiration of 20 years should the same be deemed advantgeous, and that the general council shall have the right to regulate and establish the rates of tole by law.

Approved October 12, 1848.

Thomas Lefllore.
S. D. Fisher.
Peter Folsom.

AN ACT Arbitration.

Sec. 20. *Be it enacted, &c.* That when an Arbitrator or Arbitrators are chosen by two or more persons to decide and settle any matters in controversy, it will be necessary for each person in controversy to furnish their arbitrator or an arbitrators all proofs facts and statements or any evidence they may possess finding the case, and upon impartial trial of the same by the arbitrators as well as his or their opinion and judgements rendered on the matter in controversy shall be final and binding on all the persons concerned in chosing an arbitration as if it were done in any court of justice.

But in case the arbitrators cannot agree in forming a

decision on any case before them they shall have the right of choosing an umpire whose decision shall be final and conclusive.

Be it further enacted, That a decision is rendered by an arbitrator or arbitrators on any matter in controversy, such decision shall be recorded in the nearest court.

AN ACT New emigrants to receive Annuity with the old settlers.

SEC. 21. *Be it enacted, &c.,* That the late emigrants of Choctaws to this country who have never received any benefit by the 14th article of the treaty at dancing rabbit creek in the year 1830, shall be allowed and receive annuity with the old settlers, and also participate with them all other privileges that is held by the old settlers.

By T Mckinney.

Approved October 12, 1848.

Thomas Leflore.
S. D. Fisher.
Peter Folsom.

AN ACT Respecting strays sold on credit.

SEC. 22. *Be it enacted, &c.,* That heretofore all stray property, that may be sold in the several districts of this nation, on credit be paid for at scuh a length of time set; and not paid for at the time set, the District secretary shall have the right to order the light horse-men to take such as the Dr. may have in possession and sell for cash paid down until the amount is paid.

By James Gibson.

Approved October 12, 1848.

Thomas Leflore.
S. D. Fisher.
Peter Folsom.

SESSION XVI.—1849.

AN ACT an appropriation for nieghborhood school.

SEC. 1. *Be it enacted, &c.,* That the sum of four thousand, and five hundred dollars which was allowed to the Choctaws by the Government of the United States at its last

Session of congress, being the balance due the choctaws by the chickasaws according to treaty stipulation, be and the same is hereby set apart for the support of neighborhood schools in Puckshunubbee, Pushimataha, and Moshulatubbee districts in the following manner, viz. To be expended in Puckshunubbee District the sum of twenty two hundred and fifty dollars. In Pushimataha, and Moshulatubbee Districts eleven hundred aud twenty five dollars each.

Be it further enacted, That the funds set apart shall be under the control and management of a board of neighborhood schools to consist of three persons in each district, whose duty it shall be to receive the funds from the United Staes agent, to disignate what neighborhood schools shall be patronized to employ teachers to pay the same and to report annually to the council the condition of the schools under their control and management.

Be it further enacted, That James Garland, Zadoc Harrison, and P. P. Pitchlynn be and the same are hereby appointed managers of the neighborhood schools in Puckshunubbee district.

Captain George Folsom, William McCoy and Peter Battes to be managers in Pushimataha district, and Thomas Wall Thompson Mckinney and Cornelius McCurtain in Moshulatubbee.

And be it further enacted, That the act passed in Oct. 12 1848, Sect. 22. authorizing the chiefs to appoint Trustees to superintend the management of the sabbath school funds be and the same is hereby repealed, and that the sabbath school funds together with the schools be placed under the control and management of the neighborhood school managers.

And be it further enacted, That in case of death or resignation of any of the managers of the neighborhood schools. The chief shall have power to appoint others in their plaoes.

Be it further enacted, That the board of school managers in Pushimataha district shall have power to extend the privileges granted them in this bill to any choctaw settlement within the chickasaw district if in their estimation such settlements deserve patronage from the funds under control passed both houses.

Oct. 1849.
Approved by chiefs.

Peter Folsom.
Thomas Leflore.

AN ACT public examination.

SEC. 2 *Be it enacted &c.*, That the public examinations of the Academies, and Seminaries shall come off between the 10th and 16th July and that the vacations in each institution shall be extended to the first Wednesday in October.

Passed both houses.
Oct. 1849.

Approved by chiefs.

AN ACT locating three months shops at Silas place.

SEC. 3. *Be it enacted &c.*, That the three months shop at John Robinson removed to Silas place in Puckshunubbee district.

Approved by chiefs.
Oct 9, 1849.

AN ACT witnesses to be kept separate.

SEC. 4. *Be it enacted, &c.*, That when two or more witnesses shall appear before any court of justice to testify to any case finding, before the court, it shall be the duty of the judge to order the light.horse-men to keep such witnisses separate,from each other at court until their whole testimony is taken separately, that the trial may be fair and impartial.

Proposed by Cornelius McCurtain.
Octr 9, 1849.

Approved by chiefs.

AN ACT guardian for Idiocs.

SEC. 5. *Be it enacted, &c.*, That when any person is proved to be in a State of derangement of mind or idiocs and possessed with property there shall be a guardian appointed with the same power and instructions as specified in the law passed in session 14th in the year 1847 regulating the effects and property of orphan minors.

Approved by chiefs. Octr 9, 1849.

AN ACT white men not allowed to raise any stock in the Nation.

SEC. 6. *Be it enacted, &c.*, That from and after the passage of this act, no white man who have not married a native of this nation shall ever be allowed to raise any stock with in the limits of this nation.

Proposed by T. Mckinney.

October 10, 1849.

Approved by chiefs.

AN ACT locating three months shops at James Herveys.

SEC. 7. *Be it enacted &c.*, That the three months shop established at Col. Fishers by a former law is hereby repealed and the said three months shop shall be removed and established between the Fork of Boggy near James Herveys in Pushimatalia district.

Approved by chiefs.

October 10, 1849.

AN ACT citizens interfering the light-horse in the exercise of his duties liable to be fined.

SEC. 8. *Be it enacted, &c.*, That while any of the light-horse-men are engaged in the act of destroying spirituous liquors and they or he be prevented by any person or persons in any way whatever from executing his duty such person or persons so offending shall be liable to an action in court and be made to pay a fine not less than five dollars nor exceeding ten dollars and one half of such fine so imposed shall go to the district in which such fine may be imposed, and the other half shall go to the light-horse-man who were prevented from doing his duties.

By Nich. Cochanaur.

Octr. 10 1849.

AN ACT liberating a Creek woman.

SEC. 9. *Be it enacted, &c.*, That the creek woman who is now in bondage, and in the possession of Acharcartubbee is hereby liberated and that she be allowed citizenship in this nation.

—

AN ACT the owners of stray property proveing their property within 12 months entitled to the part deposited in the District funds.

SEC. 10. *Be it enacted &c.*, That from and after the passage of this act, that all stray property that may be sold agreeable to the act passed Oct. 1843 respecting stray property that it stand in full force with the exception of that part where it says one half of the proceeds arrising from the sales of estrays shall go to the district in which such sale may take place shall be so amended as to read thus, should the owner or owners of such property find it within twelve months after it is sold shall have the right to the amount that deposited in the district funds arrising from the sales of such strays. Provided it is satisfactory proven before any judge.

Proposed by George Hudson.
October 11, 1849.

—

AN ACT each District to pay its own Ferriage accounts.

SEC. 11. *Be it enacted, &c.*, That from and after the passage of this act, that the several districts of this nation shall bear their own expenses of paying ferriage accounts that may be incurred by any light-horse-men when upon duty together wirh the witnesses and other persons that may be actually engaged with the light-horse-men.

Proposed by Nich. Coachanaur.
October 11,
Approved by chiefs.

—

AN ACT slaves committing depredation, the owners responsible.

SEC. 12. *Be it enacted &c.*, That from and after the passage of this act, when any slave or slaves shall commit any depredation on the property of any citizen in this Nation.

The owner master or mistress of any such slave or slaves shall be held accountable and responsible, and upon satisfactory proof of the same being made, the owner of such slave or slaves shall be made to pay any valuation that may be put on the amount of damages sustained, upon judgement that may be rendered in any court of justice.

Provided the damages does not exceed the value of the slave that committed the depredation.

By Nich. Coachanaur.

AN ACT any person marrying run away matches liable to be fined.

SEC. 13. *Be it enacted, &c.*, That from and after the passage of this act, that any Captain, minister of the gospel or any other person who shall marry or join together in wedlock any run away matches shall be fined twenty five dollars for every act they violate of the above law, and all such marriages shall not be considered lawful, and all fines imposed under this law shall go to the district in which such fine may be imposed.

Proposed by Danl Folsom.

October 11, 1849.

AN ACT Polygamy.

SEC. 14. *Be it enacted, &c.*, That from and after the passage of this act, that any person or persons who shall be convicted of the crime of polygamy or of living with each other in adultery shall be liable to indictment before any court in this nation and fined not exceeding twenty-five dollars nor less than ten dollars for each of such offences.

And be it further enacted That after the passage of this act, all person or persons who may be living together out of wedlock shall be compelled to be lawfully joined together or the party refusing so to do, shall be indicted and fined not less than ten dollars nor exceeding twenty-five dollars for every such offence.

And be it enacted, &c., That the informant in all such offences as above specified shall be entitled to and receive one third of the fines that may be so collected and after deducting the fees of the district Attorney the remainder shall become district funds.

By Nich. Coachanaur.

October 11, 1849.

AN ACT white man living with an Indian woman are required to marry her lawfully.

SEC. 15. *Be it enacted, &c.*, That every white man who is living with an indian woman in this nation without being lawfully married to her, shall be required to marry her lawfully or be compelled to leave the nation and for ever stay out of it.

Be it further enacted, That no white man who is under a bad character will be allowed to be united to an Indian woman in marriage in this nation under any circumstances whatever.

By Thomas Wall.

—

AN ACT citizens assisting light-horse entitled to pay.

SEC. 16 *Be it enacted, &c.*, That from and after the passage of this act. any person or persons who shall assist any light-horse-men in destroying spirituous liquors who shall act upon the call for assistance by any light-horse-men shall be entitled to and receive one dollar for every service he may render, out of any fund belonging to the district in which such service may be performed.

Oct. 11, 1849.

—

AN ACT John McGilbury allowed citizenship.

SEC. 17. *Be it enacted, &c*, That John McGilbury of the Creek Nation, is hereby allowed citizenship in this Nation.

Approved Oct. 11, 1849. *By the Chiefs.*

—

AN ACT Increasing the number of light-horse-men in Musholatubbee District.

SEC. 18. *Be it enacted, &c.*, That from and after the passage of this act, that there shall be two additional number of light-horse-men appointed in Musholatubbee District.

Approved Oct. 11, 1849, *By the Chiefs.*

—

AN ACT Gambling.

SEC. 19. *Be it enacted &c.*, That from and after the passage of this act, any person or persons who shall introduce or bring playing cards into this nation and dispose of them in any manner whatever shall be liable to an action in court, and upon satisfactory proof being made thereof shall be compelled to pay a fine of five dollars for every pack cards he may dispose of.

And be it further enacted., That any person or persons who shall be engaged in gambling in any particular name suit kind or specis of any game with cards, and when money or any other property is allured or indulged, each or all and every person so engaged shall also upon proof be compelled to pay a fine of two dollars and fifty cents for every pack of cards they may have used in gambling.

And be it further enacted, That any person or persons who shall keep or let a house room, table or any other place where gambling with cards is indulged such person or persons shall be brought to trial in court, and upon proof shall be made to pay a fine not less than five dollars nor exceeding fifty dollars as the court may determine for every house room, table or any other place where gambling is allowed with cards.

And be it further enacted. That all fines that may be imposed under the preceeding acts shall be subject to the disposition and use of district in which such fine may be imposed.

And be it further enacted, That any person or persons who shall introduce practice or be engaged in dealing or shaking the game of chuckaluck, Ronlette farro the wheel of fortune shall be arraigned before any court and upon satisfactory proof the same shall be bound to pay a fine not less than twenty five dollors nor exceeding one hundred dollars.

And be it further enacted., That if any white man be ingaged in gambling in this nation, in any of the games above specified upon complaint being made to the agent or any chiefs shall be ordered out of the nation forth with and forever to remain out of it.

And be it further enacted, That the informer against persons engaged in any of the above specified games shall be entitled to one half of the fines collected.

Nich. Coachanaur.

Octr. 11, 1849. Approved; By chiefs.

—

AN ACT the judge may not put off a trial without sufficient reason.

SEC. 20. *Be it enacted, &c.*, That unless good and sufficient reason is shown to the court no judge when exercising the duties of his office shall grant any person in suit at law to defer or postpone the holding of court to another time.

And be it further enatced, That if postponement is allowed such postponement shall not extend any further than the setting of the next court at which time the judge shall proceed to business with such facts and evidence that may be before the court.

By Sampson Folsom.

SESSION XVII.—1850.

AN ACT unmarked cattle two years old and upwards posted as other strays.

1. *Be it enacted, &c.*, From and after the passage of this act, that all unmarked cattle two years old and upward running with the cattle of any person in their range be posted as other estrays.

Proposed by George Hudson.
Approved Oct. 15th, 1850.
Geo. W. Harkins.
Cornelius McCurtain.
Geo. Folsom. *Chiefs.*
Dickson Frazier. *Speaker.*

AN ACT empowering the chief to offer rewards for the apprehension of outlawed murderers.

SEC. 2. *Be it enacted, &c.*, That the chiefs of the several districts shall have power to offer rewards for the apprehension or killing of out lawed murders and other criminals who may escape beyond reach of justice, but each reward shall not exceed fifty dollars for each outlaw, which reward shall be paid out of the national funds.

Approved Oct. 1859.
Geo. W. Harkins.
Cornelius McCurtain.
Geo. Folsom.
Chiefs.
Dickson Frazier. *Speaker.*

AN ACT Pushimataha District divided into Counties, names and boundaries.

SEC. 3. *Be it enacted, &c.*, That Pushimataha District is hereby subdivided and laid off in four Counties to be styled and named *Kiamichi* county *Tiger Spring* county, *jack's fork* county and *Shappaway* county, to be bounded as follows [viz.] the Kiamichi county line shall commece at the mouth of Kiamichi stream thence up said stream to the mouth of ten mile creek thence up stream to the ridge dividing its waters from Caney or *Arch Mcgees* creek. thence Southwest along said ridge to the said caney creek, thence down the same to the muddy fork of Boggy, thence down said stream to where the road leading from Fort Smith to Beals ferry crosses Boggy, thence along said road to Beals ferry on Red River, thence down said River to the beginning.

2. The Tiger Spring county line shall commence on Red River where the chickasaw District boundary line strikes ths same. Thence down said river to Beals ferry where the *Kiamichi* county strikes the same, thence North East along said county line to the mouth of *Caney* or *arch Mcgees* creek, thence up the main channel of the muddy fork of Boggy to where the road leading from Fort Smith to Fort Wash itaw crosses the same, thence along said road to where chick asaw District line crosses the same, thence along said District line to the beginning.

3. *The jack fork* county line shall commence on the muddy fork of Boggy, at the mouth of *caney or arch Mcgees* creek. thence up said creek along the *Kiamichi* county line to the source of ten mile creek, thence down said creek to *Kiamichi* stream thence North and West along the Pushimataha district boundary to where the same crosses the road leading from Fort Smith to Fort Washita, thence along the said road to the muddy fork or middle fork of Boggy, thence down the said stream to the beginning.

The Shappaway county line shall commence on the chickasaw district boundary, where the road leading from Fort Washitaw to Fort Smith crosses the same, thence along said road passing the Boggy depot to where it crosses the chickasaw district boundary near Brashear's, thence West and south along said District boundary to the beginning.

Approved Oct. 15th 1850.

Geo. W. Harkins

Cornelius McCurtain.

Geo. Folsom. *Chiefs.*

D. Frazier. *Speaker.*

AN ACT Chickasaw District divided into counties, names and boundaries,

SEC. 4. *Be it enacted, &c.* That the Territory within the following limits to wit. Beginning at the South East corner of the Chickasaw district running with the Eastern boundary line of Chickasaw district North to where the road leading from Fort Towson to Fort Washita crosses said line thence with said road to Fort Washita thence due West to Washita River thence down said Washita River to Red Rriver then, down Red River to the beginning shall form the county of *Ponola.*

Be it further enacted, that the Territory within the following limits to wit. Beginning at the mouth of False Whashita thence up said Washita to its source thence due North to the canadian thence up said canadian to the 100th. Degree of West longitude thence South to Red River thence down Red River to the beginning shall form a county and be called the county of Wichita

3 Be it further enacted that the territory within the following limits to wit; Beginning on the washita River at the north west corner of Ponola county, thence up said Washita river and with the Wichita county line to the cannadian River thence down said River to a point due north of low blue River thence south to said low blue River thence down said blue River to where the Chickasaw district boundary line crosses the same Thence with said line to the North East corner of Ponola county line thence West wardly along ponola county line to the beginning shall form a county to be called the county of *caddo.*

4 Be it further enacted that the territory within the following to wit: Beginning where the chickasaw district boundary crosses the low blue river and, thence up

said low blue river and with the caddo county line to the canadian thence down the canadian to the mouth of brushy creek thence up said Brushy creek to its source thence with the chickasaw boundary line to the legening shall form a county and be called the county of Perry.

AN ACT Musholetubbee District divided into counties, names and boundaries.

SEC. 5. Be it enacted &c. That Mosholatubbee district is hereby laid off into four different counties (viz) Skullyville, Sugar loaf, sam boy and gains creek county, That skullyville be bounded as follows, beginning where the state line of Arkansas crosses the arkansas river above fort smith thence up said river to the mouth of Cashier thence up said Cashier to its source Thence due straight line to the road leading from Fort Smith to Fort Washita crosses the narrow thence east wardly along on the cavinole mountain and strike the poteau about one mile above kowa homah's place thence down the channel of the Poteau to the mouth of lick creek thence up said creek to the western line of arkansas State thence due north along on the said line to the beginning.

The sugar loaf county bounded as follows, viz. Commence where skullyville county strikes the western line of arkansas state, thence due south along said line to the top of dividing ridge seperates between Puckshinabi and mosholatubbee districts thence west along said ridge to the source of gains creek thence due north to the head waters of Bayou zeal about four or five miles above Narrow. Thence down said Bayou zeal to where the boundary line of skullyville county crosses the Narrow.

The sam boy county bounded as follows (viz) Commence at the mouth of Cashier thence up arkansas river to the mouth the canadian Thence up said canadian river to the mouth of long ton creek Thence up said creek to its source thence due south to the head waters of sam boy. Thence east wardly to the source of Bayou zeal. Thence down said to where sugar loaf county strikes the creek.

The gains county to commence at the long town creek

Thence up canadian river, To the mouth of gains creek, Thence up said creek to the mouth of brushy Thence up said brushy to dividing ridge which seperate between mosholatubbee and Puckshinabbee districts, Thence east wardly along said dividing ridge to the boundary line of sugar loaf county.

Approved Oct. 16 1850.

G. W. Harkins.
Cor. McCurtain Chiefs.
D. Frazer Speaker.

AN ACT Puckshunubbee District divided into Counties names and boundaries.

SEC. 6. *Be it enacted, &c.*, Puckshunubbee district shall be divided into seven counties, (viz) Wade, Narshoba, Eagle, Red river, Towson Cedar and Boktola. Wade county shall be bounded as follows to begin on the top of the dividing ridge where the bound any of Musholatubbee district intersect the boundary line of the state of Arkansas. Thence along the top of the dividing ridge West wardly to where the road leading from horse praire to Fort Smith crosses the same, thence along said road to Jacks fork, thence down Jacks fork to its junction, thence on a straight line in a south east direction till it strikes the brow of the Kiamichi mountain, thence along the brow of said mountain eastwardly till it strikes the boundary of the state of Arkansas thence along said boundary northwardly to the beginning.

2. Narshoba County shall be bounded on the north by Wade county to a point opposite the source of little river thence on a straight line to said source, thence down liitle river to where an old hurricane crosses said river about a mile and a half above Silas Garland's, thence along said Hurricane Eastwardly to its termination, thence on a line Eastwardly to where it may strike the boundary line of the state of Arkansas five miles north of widow Solimon's, thence along said boundary line northward to the beginning.

3. Eagle county shall be bounded on the north where boktokla county strikes nashoba county, thence down yasshobok, to where it emties into little river, thence down the said river to where it crosses the Arkansas boundary line,

thence along said line till it strikes narshoba county line thence along said line to the beginning.

4. Boktokla county shall be bounded on the north by narshoba county to the point where it strikes little river, thence down said river to the mouth of yasshobok, thence up yasshobok till it strikes the boundary line of narshoba county line thence to the beginning.

5. Red River County shall begin where the boundary line of Arkansas crosses little river, thence up said river to Adam Leflore's ferry, thence south leaving said Leflore's house in towson county, thence on a direct line to Scotts old place on water-hole creek, thence down said creek to where a new road crosses the same below Zadoc Harrison's residence, thence down the new road till it strikes Red river, thence down the said river to where Arkansas line crosses Red river thence along the said line to the beginning.

6. Towson County shall be bounded as follows, viz, to begin at Adam Leflore's ferry, thence up little river till it strikes the seven brothers, thence down the said mountain till it strikes Kiamichie, thence down Kiamichie to its mouth, thence down Red river to where Red river county line strikes Red river, thence up said line till it strikes the water-hole creek, thence up the said line to the beginning.

7. Cedar County shall be bounded on the north by Wade county on the west by Kiamichie, on the south by Towson county on the east by nasshoba county.

Approved Oct. 16. 1850.

G. W. Harkins
C. McCurtain
G. Folsom

AN ACT empowering light-horse-men to search suspected places for liquar.

SEC. 7. *Be it enacted &c.* that the light-horse men of this nation are hereby authorized and empowered to search any person's house or dwellings wagon boat pack horse or any persons bag or saddle bags where they may have good reason or evidence to suspect of having any intoxicating whiskey wines or other intoxicating liquors and if found the light-horse-men shall destroy the liquor and the vessel containing the same.

Approved Oct. 16, 1850.

G. W. Harkins
C. McCurtain Chiefs.
G. Folsom.
D. Frazier Speaker.

AN ACT removing the shop at G. Pusley's to John Anderson's.

SEC. 8 Be it enacted by the general council of the choctaw nation assembled that the public shop which was formerly kept at Capt. George Pusleys be removed and the same to be established at Captain John Anderson.

Approved Oct. 16, 1850.

G. W. Harkins.
C. McCurtain *Chiefs.*
G. Folsom.
D. Frazer. Speaker.

AN ACT respecting jails.

SEC. 9. *Be it enacted, &c.*. That there shall be erected in each district one substantial jail to be located at some suitable place in each of the districts.

2. When a jail is erected in each district, it shall be and only to lodge criminals and offenders against the dignity and laws of this nation.

3. For this purpose the chief of each district shall authorize three persons to select a place and to contract for the building of a jail, but such contract shall not exceed one hundred dollars.

4. The jailor shall be the captain of the light-horse-men of the several districts, there shall be allowed three dollars per week for his attention to any prisoner or prisoners during imprisonment, but in case of sickness or inability of any of the light-horse-men to perform the duty assigned him, he shall appoint any light-horse-man to act as jailor.

Approved Oct. 1850.

George W. Harkins.
Cornelius McCurtain.
George Folsom. *Chiefs*
Dickson Frazier. *Speaker.*

AN ACT establishing a shop on Jacks fork.

SEC. 10. *Be it enacted, &c.*, That there shall be one three months shop established in Pushimataha district and the same to be located on Jacks fork at Jackson Residence.

Approved Oct. 15 1850. By James Patterson.

G. W. Harkins.
Cornelius McCurtain. *Chiefs.*
Dickson Frazier. *Speaker.*

—

AN ACT removing the shop to Colemon Cole.

SEC. 11. *Be it enacted, &c.*, That the black smith shop located at or near Edmund Mckinney's old place shall be removed to Colemon Coles, in Puckshunubbee district.

Proposed by Colemon Cole.

Approved Oct. 15, 1850.

G. W. Harkins.
Cornelius McCurtain.
George Folsom. *Chiefs.*
D. Frazier. *Speaker.*

—

AN ACT removing the joint shop to John Frazier.

SEC. 12. *Be it enacted, &c.*, That the session 14 and that portion of the section 28, relating to joint shop shall be changed so as to read thus, that the joint shop established at V. Brashears by committee shall be removed and bo located and be equal with the other three months shop at Capt. John Frazier's in Puckshunubbee district, be it further enacted that the black smith tools at or near Edmund Mckinney's old place which belong to the said district shall be taken for the use of the said shop.

Approved Oct. 15, 1850.

George W. Harkins.
Cornelius McCurtain.
George Folsom. *Chiefs.*
Dickson Frazier. *Speaker.*

—

AN ACT elections.

SEC. 13. *Be it enacted, &c.*, By the general council of the Choctaw Nation assembled that in all elections by the people the mode of voting shall be done by ballot and in the following manner. To wit Evey voter shall write out the names of such candidates as he may think proper to vote for and present the same to the judge of the election who being satisfied with the qualifications of the voter shall number the ticket which number shall correspond with the number of such voters names on the margin of the Poll book, and the judges shall deposite such ticket into the ballot box.

The clerks of the elections shall write down the names of each and every voter on the poll book numbering the same on the margin from one on to the whole number of voters that may be polled at such elections.

Names of Voters.

1	Jack.
2	Bill,
3	Tom.
4	Bully,
5	Johny.

2. The county court of each county at the term of said court, immediately preceeding each general election shall fix a place in each county at which all elections shall be held, and shall appoint three discreet persons in each county having the qualifications of elections to act as judge of the election within the county and the judges so appointed shall select two persons having the like qualification to act as clerk thereof.

3. The judges of elections appointed as aforesaid shall continue to be judge of elections within their respective counties untill the next general election.

4. If the court shall fail to fix a place at which elections are to be held in any county or to appoint judges of elections or those appointed fail to act it shall be the duty of the light-horsemen of the county to fix a place for holding the election and the voters when assembled may appoint the

judge.

5. It shall be the duty of the light-horse-men of each county at least one month before each general election to give public notice by proclamation through all the county of the time and several places of holding such elections in his county and the officers to be elected at that time.

6. A copy of such proclamation shall be set up at each of the places fixed for holding such election and at two or more of the most public places in each county.

7. The judges before entering on their duties shall take before some person authorized by law to administer oath. The following oath, I do sware that I will perform the duties of judge of this election according to law and to the best of my abilities, and that I will studiously endeavor to prevent fraud, deceit and in conducting the same.

9. The clerks of each election before entering on their duty shall take an oath that they will faithfully record the names of all voters and carry out in lines and colums of all the voters polled.

10.—In case there shall be no person present at the opening of any election authorized to adminster oaths. It shall be lawful for the Judges of the election to administer oath to each other and to the clerks and such Judges shall have full power authority to administer all oaths that may be necessary in conducting any election.

11.—The person who shall administer the oaths to the Judges and clerks of any election shall cause a certificate to be prefixed to the poll books in words to the follow ing effect. I do certify that — and Judes — and clerks of the elections held in the precincts of — and in the county of — in the district of — on the — day in the year 18 hundred and — were sworn as the law directs previous to entering on their respective duties which Certificate shall be subscribed by the person administering the oath and shall be considered as a part of the election.

12.—It shall be the duty of the clerks of the districts at least one week before each general election to make out and deliver to the light horsemen of the county two blank poll books, Ink and quills for each precinct in each county properly laid off in columes with proper captians And forms of oaths, and certificate attached thereto and such pole books shall contain a sufficient number of pages to record the names of the voters in the county.

13 It shall be the duty of the light-horse-men forthwith to deliver such books, ink and quills to the judges of the election within their respective presents in each county.

14 The judges of each election shall open the polls in the morning and the same shall close at sun down on the same day

15 The Judges of each election shall order the light-horse-men to take any person for contempt abuse or disorderly behaviour during election and shall bind him to keep the peace and impose a fine not exceeding ten dollars.

16 When any person shall offer to vote and when no one of the Judges shall be acquainted with the qualification of such person the Judges may examine him touching his qualification as an elector under oath or they may satisfy themselves in relation thereto by any other testimony.

17. Every person not being a qualified voter according to the constitution and laws of this nation. who shall vote in any election, within this nation knowing that he is not entitled to vote shall forfeit the sum of not exceeding twenty dollars to be recovered by action of law. Imposing fine before any county Judge one half for the use of the person who shall see for the same.

18 If any person shall vote more than once at any one election he shall forfeit a sum not exceeding fifty dollars and to be recovered and applied in the same manner as provides in preceeding section.

19 If any Judge or clerk of any election or any other person concerned in the conducting of any election shall neglect improperly, delay or refuse to perform any of the duties required by this act having undertaken so to do, or shall knowingly admit any to vote not qualified according to law or shall be guilty of corruption partialality or manifest misbehaviour in anything to such election or shall unduly attempt to influence the election or shall knowingly receive any improper vote, he shall forfeit and pay a sum not exceeding fifty dollars, an action damages in the name of any person who may sue for the same.

20. At the close of election, the judges shall certify under their hands, the number of votes given to each person and

the officers for which such votes were given, which shall be attested by the clerks.

21. After closing the polls and making the certificate required in the preceeding section, the judges shall enclose and seal one of the poll books together with such certificate and direct to the supreme national judge of the district, and the packet so endorsed and directed, shall be conveyed by the light-horse-men of the county to the supreme national judge of the district within three days after the close of the polls and the other poll books shall be retained by the judges free for inspection of all persons.

22. On the fifth day after the election or sooner if all the returns have been received, the supreme judge shall take to his assistance any two of the county judges, if they can be conveniently had, and if not, then two persons having the qualification of elections, and shall proceed to open and compare the several elections returned which had been made to the place of holding the circuit court in the district, and make abstracts of the votes given for the several candidates for each office on separate sheets of paper.

23. Such abstract being signed by the judge shall be deposited in the office of the clerk of the district there to remain.

24. Each judge in comparing the returns of the elections shall do it publicly in the court house, or in the place in which the circuit court is usually held, first giving notice of the same by public proclamation at the door, after comparing the votes as above stated, he shall proclaim the person having the highest number of votes elected.

25. Be it enacted, that the chiefs of the several districts shall have the power to appoint county judges, district attorney within their respective districts until the next general election. The district attorneys when elected at the next general election day shall hold their office for the term of one year, but subject to reelection—they shall hereafter receive for their services, forty dollars and such after fees as may have been heretofore provided by law.

—

AN ACT County court proceenings.

SEC. 14. *Be it enacted, &c.,* That every county judge shall have power to hear, try and determine all actions in this act, enumerated according to law and equity.

2. Every county judge shall have jurisdiction over the following actions and proceedings first for actions for trespass on the case for enquiries to person or property wherein the damages claimed does not exceed fifty dollars, second all actions for any penalty not exceeding fifty dollars given by any statute law of this nation, and third to take and enter judgement on the confession of a defendent where the amount confessed shall not exceed fifty dollars.

3. Every county judge shall have jurisdiction coextensive with the county for which he may be elected or appointed.

4. Every action cognizable before a county judge, instituted by summons or warrant, shall be tried first before a county court wherein the defendent resides or if there be one or more defendents to a suit, residing in different counties or districts, then in the county where the defendent and plaintiff both reside, and the other parties required to attend by summons or warrant as the case may be.

5. All criminal offenders against the peace and dignity of the nation, shall be tried in the county wherein such offence may be committed and all such offenders who may escape into another county in the same district, may on demand of the judge of the county from which he or she escaped to the Judge of the county in which such offender may be found, shall be apprehended and returned to the county having cognisance of the same for trial.

6.—The Judges of the connty courts shall in no case have jurisdiction to try and determine any criminal case or penal offence against the nation but may set as examing courts and commit, discharge or remand to the court having jurisdiction for further trial, offenders against the peace for the foregoing purposes they shall have power to issue all necessary process, they shall have power to bind to keep the peace, or for good behaviour.

7. The county judges may set hear and try cases that may properly come before them, but shall have the power to summon a jury of seven disinterested persons of the county to try such cases as they may deem necessary.

8. The county judges may hold their courts on any Wednesday of the week, when cases for trial present themselves at such places as may hereafter be designated by law.

9. All process issued by the county judges shall run in the name of the Choctaw Nation, dated on the day it is issued and signed by the judge granting the same.

10. The summons may be in the following form,

County of ——, } SS.
The Choctaw Nation. }

To the light-horse-men of —— County greeting, you are hereby commanded to summon to appear before the undersigned, judge of the County of —— on the — day of — at ten o'clock in the forenoon, at — in the same County, to answer in the complaint of ——; Given under my hand this day of ——. A. B. Judge.

11. Every summons shall be served at least three days before the day of appearance therein mentioned and it shall be executed first by reading the same to the defendant, or second by delivering a copy of the summons at his usual place of abode, with some free person who is a member of his family over the age of 12 years.

12. Every light-horse-man serving any process authorized by this act, shall return their —— in writing, the time and manner of service at any time before the next court, and shall sign his name to the same.

13. The judge of the county court without the consent of either party to a suit, may if necessary adjourn the cause not exceeding thirty days.

14. The judges of the county court on the application of either party on good cause shown, may adjourn a cause not exceeding thirty days for any one adjournment, and may adjourn for a longer period with the consent of both parties.

15. No adjournment shall be allowed upon the application of a party unless such party satisfy the judge by his own affidavit, or the affidavit of some other person that he cannot safely proceed to trial for want of some material testimony or witness, that he has used due diligence to obtain the same and that if an adjournment be allowed he will be able to procure such testimony or witness in time to be used on the trial.

16. A subpaena by a county judge shall be valid to compell

the attendance of a witness before such judge in the same county where the cause is to be tried or being in an adjoining county.

17. Whenever it shall appear to the satisfaction of a judge by proof made before him that any person duly subpaenaed to appear before him in a suit, shall have failed without just cause, to attend as a witness in conformity to such subpaena, and the party in whose behalf subpaena was issued or his agent shall oath that the testimony of such witness is material, the judge shall have power to issue an attachment to compell the attendance of such witness.

18. Every person duly subpaenaed as a witness who shall not appear, shall forfeit for the use of the county in which he is subpaenaed to appear, unless some reasonable excuse shall be shown on the oath of such witness or the oath of some other person—such fine not exceeding ten dollars, as the judge shall think reasonable to impose, and the judge shall make an entry in his docket of the conviction and of the cause thereof.

19. Either party to a civil suit depending before a county judge upon notice to the other party, cause the deposition of every witness therein to be taken by any judge of this nation.

20.— No such deposition shall be taken unless notice in writing of the time and place of taking the same shall have been previously served on the other party at least three days before the taking thereof.

21.—Any person aggrieved by the Judgement rendered by a county Judge and except a Judgement of nonsuit may in person or by his Agent make his appeal therefrom to the district circuit court of the same district where the Judgement was rendered.

22—No appeal shall be allowed unless the following requisites be complied with first the applicant or some person for him shall make and file with the Judge an affidavit within ten days after the Judgement was rendered setting forth that the appeal is not taken for the purpose of delay, but that justice may be done him, second the affidavit must also set forth specially, what part of the Judgment or decree of the court he may take exceptions to when all of which is complied with the Judge may grant such applicant an appeal which shall be delivered to the clerk of the circuit court at least ten days before the first day of the term of the circuit court and enter on the dacket for trial before the circuit court

23—If a county Judge fail to allow an appeal in a cause where the same ought to be allowed the circuit court on such fact satisfactorily appearing by the statement of both parties compell the Judge to allow the same and return his proceedings in the suit together with the papers requind to be returned by him.

AN ACT to organize and establish circuit courts and to define their powers and jurisdiction in law and Equity.

Sec. 1. *Be it enacted &c.*, That for the purpose of establishing a circuit court the several districts of the choctaw nation shall compose judecial districts.

2. That the judge of the circuit court shall be elected and take the oath prescribed in the constitution before entering upon the duties of his offiice.

3. That the circuit court shall be held in each district of this nation four times in each and every year and shall commence on the day, and may continue for the terms herein specified, that is to say in Puckshunubbee District first monday in Jan. April, July, and Oct. in Pushimataha District on the second monday in Jan, April, July, and October.

In chickasaw District on the third monday in Jan, April, July, and October. In Moshulatubbee District on the forth monday in Jan, April, July, and October, and may continue at each term there of four judicial days if business so long required and no longer provided also that the provision of this section shall be enforced and take effect from and after the first monday of January next.

4. The circuit court in the several districts in which it may be held shall have Jurisdiction as followe first as a court of law in all penal and criminal cases which shall not be authorized provided for by law. Second exclusive original jurisdiction in all cases personal and mixed, which shall not be cognizable before the county court. Third applate jurisdiction from all judgements and orders of the county and

probate courts, in all cases not expressly prohibited by law and shall have the superintending control over them exclusive original jurisdiction. Fourth in each district in which it may be held as a court of equity in all cases when adequate relief cannot be had by the ordinary course of proceeding at law.

5. The chiefs of the several districts shall each procure a seal for the circuit, and shall preserve and keep the same with such emblems and devises as the courts shall think proper at the expense of the Nation.

6. The impression of the seal of the court by stamp shall be sufficient sealing in all cases when sealing is required.

7. The circuit court mention in this act shall be a court of record and shall keep just and faithful record of its proceedings.

8. The circuit court shall have power to issue all writs and process which may be necessary in the exercise of its Jurisdiction according to the principles and usages of law.

9. The several light-horse-men of the District in which the circuit court is held shall attend and be subject to the orders of the circuit judge.

10. No judge of the circuit who is interested in any suit or related to either party within the fourth degree of consanguinity or affinity, or shall have been counsil in any suit or action shall set on the determination thereof without the consent of both parties.

11. The judge of the circuit court may at any time hold a special term for the trials of persons confined in jail by making a written order to that effect and transmitting it to the clerk of the court who shall enter the same on the record of court.

12. The judge shall in such order direct the clerk to issue a notice to the light-horse-men requiring him to summon a grand Jury to attend such special terms of the court.

If any person shall be confined in jail who may not been indicted.

13. When a special term of the court shall be ordered under the preceeding provisions. The judge ordering the same shall cause a notice to be served and the attorney for the district prosecuting for such circuit, Five days before

the commencement of such special terms.

14. No special terms after circuit court shall beheld within in twenty days of the regular terms of such court.

15. No writ plea or proceeding whatsoever civil or criminal shall be deemed discontinued or abated by the failure of any term or session of the court nor boy the failure to enter a continuance of any suit or cause on the record, but the same be continued and proceeded as if no such failure had happened.

16. The circuit court shall have power to punish as for criminals contempt persons guilty of the following act, and no others: 1st disorderly, contempteous or insolent behavior during its settings in its immediate view and present and directly to interrupt its proceeding or to impair the respect due to its authority: second any breach of the peace or disturbance directly and tending to interrupt its proceedings. Third wilful disobedience of any process order lawfully issued or made by its fourth continuances and unlawful refusal of any person to be sworn as a witness and when sworn the like refusal to answer any legal and proper interrogatory.

17. Punishment for contempt may be by fine or imprisonment in the jail of the district, when the courts may be setting or both in the discression of the court but the fine shall in no case exceed the sum of fifty dollars nor the imprisonment ten days, courts shall always have power to imprison until their adjournment.

18. The several light-horse-men are authorized and required to furnish the fuel which may be necessary for the use of court and the clerks shall furnish all blank books and stationary for the use of the same at the expenses of the district.

19. The circuit court shall audit and adjust the accounts of the clerks for expenditures made under this act and certify the balance accordingly.

20. The auditor of public accounts in caeh district shall draw his warrant for the amount of such expenditures, and the certificates of the court shall be a sufficient voucher.

21. In all appeals from the circuit to the supreme national shall be applied for and granted during the term and which the decision complained of is made.

22. In all proceedings under this act not before enumerated the order or the decision of the circuit court shall be final and conclusive unless good cause or fraud be shown.

23 In all cases where appeals are allowed the party appealing, by his agent or attorney may tender to the court a bill of exceptions espicially setting forth each item the allowance rejection of which is objected to and the decision of the court and if such statement be time the judge of the circuit shall sign the same.

24. When such appeals shall be granted or taken the clerk at the court shall transmit to the supreme national court a certified transcript the record and proceedings relating to the matter appealed from together with the original papers in his office relating to the decision excepted to.

25. On every appeal from county the circuit court shall determine the points made to the decision to which exception have been filed and if the circuit court should be of opinion that the county court erred in relating to any meterial question of law or fact the circuit court shall try and determine the matter in question, and such court shall make order and decision that have been made by the county court.

26. The circuit court shall cause its judgement and decision to be certified to the county court which shall be entered of record as the decision, order or judgement of such court.

27. All final decisions judgements and decrees rendered in the circuit court shall be carried into execution by the light-horse-men by order of the judges.

Approved Oct. 16, 1850.

G. W. Harkins.
Cornelius McCurtain.
George Folsom. *Chiefs.*
Dickson Frazier. *Speaker.*

Sec. 16. **AN ACT** to establish and organize the Supreme National court, and define the powers and jurisdiction there of.

1. *Be it enacted*, by the general Council of the Choctaw nation assembled that from and after the passage of this act, the Supreme national court shall commence and be holden

on the first Wednesday in November and may in the year 1851 in each and every year thereafter at the seat of government.

2. The Supreme court in cases not especially provided for by constitution shall in all matters of law have jurisdiction only of appeals from judgement decision, and in all matters in equity of appeals from the judgement decrees and orders of the circuit.

3. Such courts shall have power to direct the form of writs and process, not being contrary to or inconsistent with the constitution and laws of this nation.

4. In all appeals and bills of exception the supreme court shall examine the record award a trial, reverse or affirm the judgement or decision of circuit court or give such judgement as such court ought to have given as may seem agreeable to law and equity.

5. No judge of the Supreme court who is interested in any suit or related to either party within the fourth degree of consanguinity or affinity or shall have been of council in any suit or action shall set on the determination thereof without the consent of parties.

6. The supreme court shall appoint its own clerk who shall hold his office for the term of four years, and shall keep his office at the place where said court may hold its term.

7. The supreme court shall in term time call upon one or more light-horse-men of the district to wait and attend to the execution of orders or decrees of said court.

AN ACT regulating the manner of drawing jurors for the several courts of the several districts of this nation.

SEC. 17. *Be it enacted*, by the general council of the choc taw nation assembled, that from and after the passage of this act, that it shall be the duty of the judge to furnish to the district clerk of their respective districts the names of per sons who are competent to serve as jurors which list shall be furnished in writing.

SEC. 2. *Be it enacted &c.*, that the list of names so taken and furnished the district clerk, shall be set down by him in a book kept for that purpose. Also set down names on a separate strip of paper and put them into a box to be kept by him marked number one. [No. 1]

Sec. 3. There shall be drawn from said box by the clerk and captain of the light.horse-men or any one them alternately thirty names in open court. For the districts of Moshulatubbee, Pushimataha and Chickasaw and forty two for the district of Apuckshunubbee.

Persons to serve as jurors in their respective district circuit court according to law, That immediately after the requisite number of jurors shall be drawn in the manner prescribed by this act. The clerk of the court shall issue a notice to the jurymen returnable to the next term of said court.

4. It shall be the duty of the light-horse-men at least ten days before the next term of court. Summon the jurors named in such notice either by giving them personal notice at their usual place of abode in the hands of some member of the family over 12 years of age notifying him to attend according to such summons.

5. Any juror being summoned as aforesaid who shall fail to attend shall be liable to a fine not exceeding ten dollars nor less than five dollars unless good cause be shown to the judge on or before the next term of the court.

6. From the number of jurors summoned as aforesaid and attending any circuit court, there shall be drawn by lot seven persons who shall constitute the grand Jury to serve during the term for wich they are summoned who shall be sworn to inquire into and present to the district attorney all treasons murders felonies or other misdemeanor against the laws of this nation within their respective districts.

7. From the whole number of the grand Jury the court shall appoint a foreman and the concurrence of two thirds out of the six shall in every case be necessary for the indictment of any person for violationg the laws of this nation.

8. The grand Jury when setting for that pupose shall have power to summon any person or persons as witness againts offenders againts the laws of this nation.

And the light-horse-men shall be subjected to their orders to cause the attendance of such witnesses.

9. That the remaining jurors after the grand Jury shall have been drawn as required in this act, shall constitute the

petit Jury and set for the trial of all cases that may come before the circuit court at the time for which they were summoned to attend under the following rules and regulations [viz.] The names of the Petit Jury shall be written down and the clerk shall first present the list to the defendent, who shall object to one Juryman. Then the plaintiff to another and so on alternately till the number is reduced to twelve persons who shall sit for the trial and determination of the case for which they were chosen provided either or both parties may object to two additional Jurymen, by assigning such reason as the court may deem sufficient in which case the Judge shall order the light-hors-men to summon a sufficient number of disinterested men to serve in the place of those that may be objected to.

10. The concurrence of all the twelve jurors who may sit to try any case shall be necessary to a decision.

AN ACT pay of county judges.

Sec. 18. *Be it enacted* by the general council of the choctaw nation assembled. That county Judges of the several districts of this nation shall receive for their services forty dollars per annum. Together with such perquisites and fees as may be here in after provided by law.

And the law heretofore existing allowing the inferior Judge a compensation of thirty dollars a year, be and the same is hereby repealed.

Approved Oct. 16, 1850.

AN ACT removing the three months shop to Nelson McCoy.

Sec. 19. *Be it enacted &c.*, that the three months public shop at Kully Kashaha shall be removed and located at Nelson McCoy's in Puckshunubee district.

Proposed by G. Hudson.

Approved Oct. 16. 1850.

AN ACT Sodomy.

Sec. 20. *Be it enacted, &c.*. That when any person or persons be convicted of committing sodomy shall suffer death for the first offence to be determined by twelve Jurors and excuted according to law.

Approved Oct. 17, 1850.

—

AN ACT against murdering a murderer in custody.

Sec 21. *Be it enacted, &c.*, that from and after the passage of this act, that if any person or persons shall in any way murder or put to death a murderer or other person who may be in custody at the time, such offenders shall be esteemed guilty of murder and be proceeded against as such, if convicted shall suffer death as provided by law in such cases.

Proposed by J. Wall.

Approved Oct. 17. 1850.

—

AN ACT of National judges and circuit judges.

Sec. 22. *Be it enacted, &c*, That the judges of the supreme national court of this nation shall be allowed and receive one hundred dollars each per annum. Be it further enacted that the judge of the circuit court shall be allowed and receive four hundred dollars per annum, to be paid out of the national fund, the chickasaw district paying her fourth part of said sum.

Approved Oct. 17 1850.

—

AN ACT providing an additional light-horse-man in Mosholatubbee district.

Sec 23. *Be it enacted &c.* That there shall be an additional light-horse-man appointed in Mosholatubbee district and whose salary will be the same as those provided for by law to be paid out of the funds belonging to the nation.

Approved Oct. 17, 1850.

—

AN ACT providing an additional light-horse-man in Pushimataha district.

Sec. 24. *Be it enacted &c* That there shall be one additional light-horse-man allowed to Pushimataha district whose duties and pay shall be the same as other light-horse-men in said district.

Approved Oct. 17, 1850.

—

AN ACT locating a three months shop at Parkers

SEC. 25. *Be it enacted &c.* That there shall be a three months shop established at Parker in Puckshanubbe district
Approved Oct. 17. 1850.

—

AN ACT providing an additional light-horse-men in Puckshanubbee District.

SEC. 26. *Be it enacted &c.* That there shall be four additional light-horse men appointed in the district of Puckshanubbee to be paid out of the nation funds.
Approved Oct. 1850.

—

AN ACT locating the circuit court gound in Pushimataha District.

27. Be it enacted. &c. That the circuit court ground in Pushimataha district, be and is hereby located at Charles F. Stewarts.

Approved Oct. 17, 1850.

—

AN ACT Judges and preachers of the Gospel to solemnize the rites of matrimony.

SEC. 28. *Be it enacted &c.* That from after the passage of this act, It shall be lawful for all the judges of this nation and preachers of the Gospel to solemnize the rites of matrimony and issue certificates thereof if required and be allowed and receive for every such service two dollars to be paid by the parties so joined together, and be it further enacted that the law passed in session 5 section 3rd so far as relates to the fees be and is hereby repealed.

Approved Oct. 17, 1850.

—

AN ACT marriage at what age to be contracted.

SEC. 29. *Be it enacted &c.* That from and after the passage of this act, Every male who shall have arrived at the age of eighteen years, and every female who shall have arrived at the full age of sixteen years shall be capable in law of contracting marriage. But if under these ages their marriage shall be void unless free consent by the parents and relations or guardian have been obtained.

Be it further enacted that whoever shall contract marriage in fact, contrary to the prohibition of the preceeding section of this act, and whoever shall knowingly solemnize the same shall be deemed guilty of high misdemeanor, and shall upon conviction be fined or imprisoned at the discretion of the court.

Approved Oct. 1850.

SESSION XVIII—Nov. 8, 1851.

AN ACT pay of county court jurymen.

Sec. 1. *Be it enacted &c.* That the jurymen of the county courts of this nation, be allowed fifty cents on every case they may be called to sit.

Approved Nov. 14, 1851.

AN ACT general annuity of 3,000 dollars made national fund.

Sec. 2. *Be it enacted &c.* That the three thousand dollars secured to the Choctaws by the treaty with the United States of 1805, be made a national fund for defraying the expenses of the Districts, after the annuity of 1851.

And be it further enacted that the chiefs pay be made therefrom. Approved Nov. 14, 1851.

AN ACT salary of Chiefs.

Sec. 3. *Be it enacted &c.* That each District Chief shall receive annually, two hundred and fifty dollas as their salaries. Approved Nov. 14, 1851.

AN ACT Blue county court.

Sec. 4. *Be it enacted &c.* That the Blue County Court Ground, be at the edge of the Prairie, one mile east of William Sueas on the road leading from his house to Armstrong Academy. Approved Nov. 14, 1851.

AN ACT Chowahla county court and election ground.

Sec. 5. *Be it enacted &c.* That the County Court Ground of Chowala in Puckshanubbee District, shall be located about one quarter of a mile south of Coleman Cole's in conjunction with the election ground.

Approved Nov. 14, 1851.

AN ACT Circuit Court, Chickasaw District.

Sec. 6. *Be it enacted &c.* That the Circuit Court of the Chickasaw District, shall hereafter be held at Post Oak Grove, and the law directing it to be held at Boiling Spring be hereby repealed. Approved Nov. 14, 1851.

AN ACT Sculliville county court and election ground.

Sec. 7. *Be it enacted &c.* That the County Court of Sculliville County in Mosholatubbee District, shall be held at the old Holitvsha Court Ground. And be it further enacted that the election shall also be held at the same place.

Approved Nov. 14, 1851.

AN ACT Samboy county court.

Sec. 8. *Be it enacted &c.* That Samboy County Court Ground in Mosholatubbee District be located at Cold Spring near the three months shop in said county.

Approved Nov. 14, 1851.

AN ACT Towson county court.

Sec. 9. *Be it enacted &c.* That from and after passage of this act, that the County Court Ground of Towson County, be and is hereby located at the Annuity Ground.

Approved Nov. 14, 1851.

AN ACT Jacksfork county court.

Sec. 10. *Be it enacted &c.* That the County Court Ground of Jacksfork County, be located at or near Amoshotubbi's house. Approved Nov. 14, 1851.

AN ACT Wade county court.

Sec. 11. *Be it enacted &c.* That from and after the passage of this act, that Wade County Court Ground, be and the same is hereby located at George McDonald's house.

Approved Nov. 14, 1851.

AN ACT Pay of light-horse-men.

Sec. 12. *Be it enacted &c.* That from and after passage of this act, That the captains of the light-horse-men of the several districts be allowed the sum of eighty-five dollars per year. And the other light-horse-men, the sum of seventy five dollars per year for their services.

Approved Nov. 14, 1851.

AN ACT pay of the clerks of National Court.

SEC. 13. *Be it enacted &c.* That the clerks of the National Court, be allowed tho sum of thirty dollars for his services.

Approved Nov. 14, 1851.

AN ACT Forbiding any person to settle within one mile of the Chickasaw boarding school.

SEC 14. *Be it enacted &c.* That from and after the passage of this act, No person shall be allowed to settle within one mile of the Chickasaw Boarding school on Washita, in Chickasaw District.

And be it further enacted, that the chief of said District when notified of such intension, by the Superintendent of said school, shall have to remove or cause to be removed all such person or persons violating this act.

Approved November 14, 1851

Proposed by M. Frazier.

AN ACT Eagle County Court and election ground.

SEC. 15. *Be it enacted*, by the General Council of the Choctaw Nation assembled. That the *County Court* of *Eagle County* in Puckshunnubbee District shall be held at *Col. Pitchlynn old place*. near eagle Town. And be it further enacted, that the election for that precinct shall be held at the same place.

Approved November. 15, 1851.

Proposed by Colemon Cole.

AN ACT pay of the members, Chiefs and clerks to the General Council.

SEC. 16. *Be it enacted*, by the General Council of the Choctaw Nation assembled. That the General Council members, Chiefs and clerks be allowed the sum of thirty five dollars each And be it further enacted, that they be allowed in addition, three cents per mile, going to, and from the Council.

Approved November, 15, 1851

—

AN ACT Red River County Court and election ground.

SEC. 17. *Be it enacted*, by the General Council of the Choctaw Nation assembled. That the *County Court Ground* of *Red River County*, be located near *George Turnbull's* old place, where the County Court has been held, and that the election in said County be held at the same place.

Approved November 1851.

Proposed by John Lake.

—

AN ACT General Council removed to Nanih Waiya.

SEC. 18. *Be it enacted &c.*, That hereafter the meeting of the General Council shall be held annually at Nanih Waiya on the first Wednesday in November, and the law directing it to be held in Doaksville is hereby repealed.

Approved November 15, 1851

—

AN ACT Sugar Loaf County Court and election ground.

SEC. 19. *Be it enacted, &c*, That the *County Court* of *Sugar Loaf County* in Moshulatubbee District, be held at *Beloved Court Grouud.* And be it further enacted that the elections be held at *Campers Schools*, in said County.

Approved Nov. 15, 1851.

Proposed by Stephen Holston.

—

SEC. 20. *Be it enacted* by the General Council of the Choctaw Nation assembled; that from and after the passage of act. There shall be established a County Court on Muddy Boggy mount Prairie, to be called mount Prairie Court in Shapawa County Pushimataha District.

Approved November. 15, 1851

Proposed by Sam Worcester.

—

AN ACT Gains County Court and election ground.

SEC. 21. *Be it cnacted, &c.*, That the County Court for Gains County in Moshulatubbee District be held at the three months shop in said County to be termed Big Lick Court. And be it further enacted that the place of holding election in said County, shall be at Post Oak Grove.

Approved November 15, 1851.

Proposed by Wm. Cass.

AN ACT Witchita County Court.

SEC. 22. *Be it enacted, &c.*, That the County Court Ground of Witchita County be located at or near Tushekias house. Approved November, 15, 1851.

Proposed by Jas. T. Gains.

AN ACT Circuit Court. Moshulatubbee District.

SEC. 23. *Be it enacted, &c.*, That the place of holdiug the Circuit Court in Moshulatubbee District, shall be located at Good Water.

Approved November, 15, 1851.

AN ACT Ponola County Court.

SEC. 24. *Be it enacted, &c.*, That the County Court of Ponola County, be located at or near Capt. Isaac Abertson old place, on the road leading from Fort Washita to Preston, and be called Albertsons Court Ground.

Approved November 15, 1851.

AN ACT election Ground in Shapawa County.

SEC. 25. *Be it enacted, &c.*, That the place of elections in Shapawa County in Pushimataha District shall be at the County Court Ground, established by law in said County.

Approved November. 15, 1851

AN ACT election Ground in Blue County.

26. *Be it enacted, &c.*. That the place of holding elections in Blue County in Pushimataha District shall be located at the County Court Ground, established by law in said County.

Approved November, 15, 1851.

Proposed by Wm. Lucas.

AN ACT empowering the chiefs to make contracts for hauling public iron.

SEC. 27. *Be it enacted, &c.*, That from and after the

passage of this act, That the chiefs of the several Districts or this Nation shall be vested with full power to make all contracts relative to hauling public iron, smith tools and also to the hire of shops within their respective Districts. And be it further enacted, that the said chiefs be required to present such contracts at every session of the General Council for appropriation to be made thereof. And be it further enacted that all such contracts shall be made at the lowest bid.

Approved November, 15 1851.

—

AN ACT Perry County Court and election Ground.

SEC. 28. *Be it enacted, &c.*, That the place of holding the County Court and elections in Perry County Chickasaw District, be at Perry Court Ground in said County.

Approved November. 15, 1851.

Proposed by Winchister Colbert.

—

AN ACT Kiamichi County Court and election Ground.

SEC. 29. *Be it enacted, &c.*, That the County Court of Kiamichi County of Pushimataha District, be held at Bok Falaya school house. And be it further enacted that the elections be held at the same place.

Approved November 15, 1851

Proposed by David McCoy.

—

AN ACT election Ground in Jacksfork County.

SEC. 30. *Be it enacted, &c*, That the place of holding elections in Jacksfork County in Pushimataha District be located at the County Court Ground established by law in said County.

Approved November, 15, 1851.

Proposed by M. Fnazier.

—

AN ACT election Ground of Witchita County.

SEC. 31. *Be it enacted, &c.*, That from and after the passage of this act, the election Grouud of Witchita County be at Tushekias Court Ground.

Approved November 17. 1851.

Proposed by Jas. T. Gains.

AN ACT Bok Tuklo County Court and election Ground.

SEC. 32. *Be it enacted &c.*, That the County Court of Bok Tuklo County, and the elections be held at or near Captain Ishtayas place in Puckshunubbee District.

Approved November 17, 1851.

Proposed by Pickens.

AN ACT Circuit Court of Puckshunubbee District and election Ground for Towson County.

SEC. 33. *Be it enacted, &c.*, That the Circuit Court of Puckshunubbee District be held at Hohtak. And be it further enacted that the lections for Towson County be held at the Annuitty Ground, where the Towson County Court Ground is establised by law.

Approved November 17, 1851.

AN ACT Nashoba county court and election.

SEC. 34. *Be it enacted. &c.*, That the County Court and election in Nashoba County in Puckshunubbee District be held at the three months shops in said County.

Approved November, 17, 1851.

Proposed by Bushpotapa.

INDEX.

SESSION X—1843.

SESSION XI—1844.

SESSION XII—1845.

SESSION XIII—1846.

SESSION XVI—1847.

SESSION XV—1848.

SESSION XVI—1849.

SESSION XVII—1850.

SESSION XVIII—1851.